PEOPLE OF THE NATIVITY

PEOPLE
OF THE
NATIVITY

Living the Christmas Story
✷ *Then and Now* ✷

MARCI ALBORGHETTI

TWENTY
THIRD 23rd
PUBLICATIONS
NEW LONDON, CT 06320
WWW.23RDPUBLICATIONS.COM

TWENTY-THIRD PUBLICATIONS
A Division of Bayard
One Montauk Avenue, Suite 200
New London, CT 06320
(860) 437-3012 or (800) 321-0411
www.23rdpublications.com

ISBN: 978-1-58595-918-1
Library of Congress Control Number: 2013945642
Printed in the U.S.A.

Contents

Introduction

FOR CHRISTIANS, THE EVENTS LEADING TO AND EN-
COMPASSING JESUS' BIRTH FORM THE MOST DRAMATIC,
BEAUTIFUL, AND BREATHTAKINGLY EXCITING NARRA-
TIVE OF OUR FAITH. In the twelve to fourteen months
preceding Jesus' birth, everything comes together. All
of history has been straining, as if itself in childbirth
pangs, toward this time. From Gabriel's announcement to
Zechariah in the temple, to the shepherds rushing down
into Bethlehem to see the newborn Messiah, this is a time
of mystery, awe, and joy.

In our tradition we "telegraph" these months into the
four weeks of Advent plus Christmas Eve. Advent is our
time of preparation, our time of hope, our time of wait-

ing. But sometimes we can get a little too caught up in the "our, our, our, we, we, we, me and mine" aspect of Advent and Christmas. We can forget that the events that became the origin story of Christianity happened, not to "us, us, us," but to real, living people in real, historical time. They happened to people who'd been waiting a lot longer than a month for the Messiah.

If the fact of Christ's birth and the events leading to it are wonderful to us, imagine what they meant to those who experienced them!

And that is just what this book does. It imagines what the events we celebrate annually meant to those who lived through them. This Nativity story allows us to step out of our own traditions and rituals and busy-ness, and into the lives of those who fulfilled their roles in the coming of God's Word-Made-Flesh. Without the people who speak in this book, the Christmas we celebrate might be a very different thing. Without these people, who did God's bidding—or, in one case, did everything possible to oppose God's bidding—our religious experience might be a very different one.

These were the months when God literally reached down and intervened in the world of humans, the world of nature, the world of politics, the world of religions, the world of racial and ethnic and social divisions. God spoke, and one of the most cynical, pagan, political leaders of the world, Caesar, called for the census that would bring Joseph and his pregnant young wife to Bethlehem. God touched the heavens with a new light, and the magi packed their bags. God whispered of religious prophecy, and Herod and the Pharisees trembled in terror and envy. God told his angels to sing, and the lowliest of all humans received the most divine of all news. These were the months when God prepared the world for a change in his relationship with it. The Creator was preparing to know his creation more deeply, more intimately, by joining them.

Imagine that!

One

ANNA & JOACHIM

The angel said to her, "Do not be afraid, Mary, for you have found favor with God. And now, you will conceive in your womb and bear a son, and you will name him Jesus." LUKE 1:30–31

"*WHAT ARE YOU SAYING?*"

Anna stared at her daughter in disbelief. Had she understood Mary's words? No, of course not. She must have heard wrong. Had the child lost her senses? She gave Mary a stern, searching glance, but her normally obedient and acquiescent daughter returned the look steadily. Without blinking. Even boldly!

"Answer me!" Anna cried, trying to keep the fear out of her voice. "What are you telling me?"

"You heard me, Mother," Mary said quietly but without hesitation. "And when the angel saw my fear and uncertainty, he said that the child *'will be great, and will be called the Son of the Most High, and the Lord God will give to him the throne of his ancestor David. He will reign over the house of Jacob forever, and of his kingdom there will be no end'* [Luke 1:32-33]. Then, when I questioned the angel about how this could happen to me, who had known no man, he told me that I would conceive the child by the power of the Holy Spirit. Those were his words, Mother."

Anna struggled to breathe as she leaned heavily on the table for support. Her eyes darted from her daughter to the open windows of their home. Quickly she rose to pull in the shutters, closing out most of the light and air. But that didn't matter now. Though she'd seen no one outside, Nazareth was a small village where everyone knew everyone else's business. This business she wanted no one to know. She sunk down again slowly across from her daughter, who sat calmly, meeting her mother's frightened gaze fearlessly. Though the room was now dim, Mary seemed to glow, causing Anna to doubt her own sanity for a moment.

"Child!" she exclaimed in a hoarse, ragged whisper. "Do you know what you are saying? Such a thing cannot be! Are you ill, Mary? Have I been working you too hard? Perhaps you should lie down and rest for a bit?"

But Mary just smiled. "Mother, his words have come true. He came to me many weeks ago, and I myself did not know what to think, so I said nothing. But it has come to pass. I carry a child!"

Anna covered her own mouth with her hands as her eyes widened. For the first time she noticed the slight swell of her slender daughter's body. Anna's strong fingers flew from her face to Mary's hands and she gripped them fiercely. "What have you done, Mary?" she groaned in despair. "You are betrothed! Joseph accepted that you would live with your father and me for another year before bringing you to his home. We asked for this because you are so young. And now this!"

"I have not betrayed Joseph, Mother, or you, or Father," Mary answered, still smiling gently.

It was the smile that truly horrified Anna. The peace she saw in Mary was incomprehensible. What had come over this child, the one all her neighbors envied her of? For Mary was—had been—the perfect daughter. What had happened to her? God forbid, had she been attacked? Had the shock robbed her of her wits and all her sense? How did I not see this? Anna asked herself. How did I fail to protect my daughter from this? Did I not raise her properly? Did I not teach her well?

Anna could barely bring herself to think about her husband, Mary's father. What would Joachim think? What would he do?

Anna couldn't help herself. "Mary, you can be stoned for this! You know the Law of Moses!"

Mary leaned forward until her face was nearly touching Anna's, until Anna could smell her daughter's familiar sweet breath and feel the warmth of her and see her dark eyes glowing so warmly.

"I will not be stoned for following the will of the Lord. The angel told me something else, Mother. He told me that our cousin Elizabeth is pregnant in her old age, even though she was barren."

"Mary! That means nothing, as you know. We've had word from Zechariah that she is with child. What you claim this angel told you is nothing that we do not know."

Mary looked at her steadily. "He told me days before we had the message from Zechariah."

Anna stared at her.

"Mother? Can you not believe me?"

Fifteen years ago, Mary's father had said these same words to Anna. She had been despondent over her failure to bear Joachim a child. They had been married for years and were advancing in age, and yet she had not been able to conceive. Joachim had never wavered in his love for her or in his hope that some day, some day, they would be parents. But she, Anna, had all but given up. She had seen the looks of the others in Nazareth, the looks of pity and, from some, the glares of suspicion. What had she done, these seemed to ask with their eyes, to cause God to punish her so severely? Why was she barren? they seemed to question, and that question was an accusation. It was believed by many of the Jews that no good woman would be denied a child from the Lord God, especially one who was trying so desperately to have a child. Had she sinned? Or had her parents sinned? Or had Joachim sinned? What caused her to be without child for so long? That is what some of her neighbors seemed to ask without saying a word. Others simply felt sorry for her, as though she were a useless dog reliant upon her master's kindness for even a bit of food. Even members of her family had urged her to give thanks that Joachim hadn't had her put away so that he could take a wife who would bear him sons.

She had come back from the well that day weeping after encountering two neighboring women, both younger than she and both having brought their children along with them. No one had said a word of condemnation to Anna, but it had broken her heart and spirit to see the love and pride those two young mothers had in their lively children. One of the oldest boys, though still too little to help, had tried to carry one of the water jugs for his mother. Unable to hold back the tears, Anna had fled home without filling her own water vessels.

Joachim had found her there. Never once in all their years together had he made her feel ashamed or inadequate. Never once had he showed her that he loved her less, and indeed, she knew he loved her more each year. Never once had he reprimanded her or repeated to her what the others must have said to him. And never once had he stopped believing that God would give them a child. Nor did he at that moment when he found her weeping.

"Anna, my beloved wife, why do you cry? You know that God is good. He will deal with us kindly. He has given us each other, has he not?" Joachim took her hand and looked into her face. "Anna? Can you not believe me?"

Beyond the reach of his consolation and his hope, she had begun to protest, "But every year that passes..."

"...means nothing!" Joachim declared, now taking both her hands in his. "Have you forgotten our ancestors? Have you forgotten how long Sarah and Abraham waited for Isaac; how Sarah foolishly laughed when the visitors from God told Abraham she would bear a son? Or how desperately Jacob and Rachel prayed before they were given Joseph and Benjamin? Don't you remember the sorrow of your namesake, Hannah, before Samuel was born to her? And Naomi! She lost two grown sons and all her future hopes, naming herself 'mara' for her bitterness, before she gained a new life and a new son through Ruth. And from thence came our greatest king, David! Our history is filled with women who waited upon God to bear children who would be the most powerful before God. The Lord God will do the same for us!"

"How can you believe this," Anna had burst out bitterly, "when everyone else thinks that I am ill-favored in God's sight?"

"God does not pay attention to foolish superstitions, and neither should you," Joachim said firmly. "We will continue to pray together for a child and trust in the Lord's goodness."

That is what they had done, and in the doing Anna had changed. She came to feel more at peace with herself and found it easier to ignore those who would scorn her with their looks and whispering. She and Joachim prayed fervently each day that God's will for them would be a child, and Anna grew calm in the love of her husband and in trusting God.

Within two years, Mary had been born. Anna had been exultant when she found she'd conceived, and she and Joachim spent those months in joyous anticipation, praising God constantly. Those in Nazareth who had pitied and derided Anna were silenced, and now when Anna met their gazes steadily, it was they who were forced to look away. When Mary was born, they took note of the fact that God had not favored them with a son, but Joachim paid no attention to any of them. He was too happy. When he came to Anna and Mary after the birth, Anna was holding her daughter blissfully. Still, she felt she must say softly in a voice weakened by the birth, "Husband, I have not given you a son. The midwife says there will not be another chance..."

Joachim lifted the quiet, pretty infant into the air, laughing. "A son!? Who needs a son when there are daughters as beautiful as mine? We are a people of strong women! Was Rebecca a son when she secured the birthright for our father Jacob? Was Miriam a son when she led all of Israel in a song of praise after God preserved us from the Egyptian army? Was Judith a son when she destroyed the most powerful general in the world and saved her people from devastation? Was Deborah a son when she judged rightly for all our people? I don't need a son. I am surrounded by the two women God has given me, and I rejoice!"

From the moment of her birth, Mary had been the delight of Joachim's eye. He lavished attention and love on her, and the others in Nazareth might have laughed at him were it not for the clear joy he took in the little girl. Anna had known immediately that she would have to be the one to discipline her daughter because Joachim would be incapable of it. And yet, Mary never seemed to require such discipline.

She was a lovely, quiet baby who never fussed and seemed content to be with her parents. "It is as though she knows we are older and must be treated gently," Anna said, only half-joking. Even as she grew into a toddler and young girl, she was sweet and attentive, knowing without being told what to do and what was right. "I have known students of Moses who find it more difficult to follow the law than my daughter," Joachim would boast.

But Anna observed her child closely. Mary was too young to know the law, and yet she never strayed into sin. It was not a fear of the law—and it was certainly not a fear of being punished by her indulgent father—that caused Mary to behave so well. Anna realized that there was a kindness in her daughter not found in many adults, never mind children. Mary had an instinct for avoiding any action that would harm or cause pain to another. Indeed, she was often doing good in childlike ways that left the law behind.

Anna recalled a time when Mary was about seven years old and they were visiting their cousins Elizabeth and Zechariah in the hills of Judea. Elizabeth was old enough to be Mary's mother, and because she herself had no child, she doted on Mary. Seeing Elizabeth talk and play with Mary, Anna had to force herself not to be jealous. *She is without her own child*, Anna reminded herself. *I, of all people, should know what that is like. I should pity her and banish this envy.* So when Elizabeth asked if she could take Mary to gather herbs, Anna, seeing the sadness and hope in her cousin's eyes, agreed.

When they returned several hours later, Mary ran to kiss her mother and then nestled in Joachim's lap. Elizabeth followed the girl with her eyes, but she was strangely quiet. They were accompanied by an older neighbor, Dina, who had gone with them for the herbs, and who was anything but quiet.

"I've never seen such a thing!" Dina declared, staring at Mary with irritation. Anna found herself annoyed at the loud woman, but also interested in spite of herself. Had her daughter actually misbehaved? She almost looked forward to discovering that Mary might have been a little mischievous, a little more like most children. Joachim, unwilling to hear or believe anything negative about his daughter, glared at Dina. She understood his look and said, "Fine, then, you do not want to hear from me? Ask Elizabeth. Ask your cousin if she has ever seen such a thing!"

Elizabeth had been gazing at Mary, but now she looked away. Anna began to be concerned. "Elizabeth?" she spoke gently. "What has happened?"

"It was nothing," Elizabeth said softly.

"Nothing!?" snorted Dina.

Elizabeth took a deep breath and started again. "It was nothing *wrong*," she said, looking pointedly at Dina. "Mary saw a coin along the path…"

"A coin?" crowed Dina. "Not just a coin, but a denarius! A full day's wages!"

Elizabeth tried to ignore her. "She found a denarius, and she wouldn't go on until she had asked everyone in the area whether they'd lost it."

"She made us knock on doors!" Dina was too appalled to contain herself. "I'm surprised no one snatched it from her hands!"

"But they didn't," Elizabeth persevered. "And I told Mary she may keep it without worry."

Anna glanced at her daughter. During all this she had nestled against Joachim, her eyes closed and her head upon his breast as though the only thing she cared to listen to was his heart beating. Joachim's eyes were on Elizabeth.

Dina interrupted again. "But did she keep it? Did she bring it home to give to her father as a dutiful daughter should?"

Anna saw Elizabeth make an effort to control herself before continuing. "On the way back from the fields, we passed a family." Dina drew breath to speak but Elizabeth gave her an angry look and the older woman clamped her teeth together and waited.

"A Samaritan family," Elizabeth added. "The woman had many children, all thin, all poorly dressed. They did not look at us, and we would have passed silently, except that Mary reached out to the woman. Mary took her hand." Elizabeth refused to acknowledge Dina's gasp. "And into her hand, Mary dropped the denarius. Then we came home. That is all."

"*All?! All?!*" Dina cried. "Instead of doing her duty and

bringing the money to her father, she gives such a sum to them, to those…"

"Enough!" Joachim spoke. "We have heard enough from you. This is not to do with you."

Dina gave him an outraged look and then strode out of the house. No doubt, thought Anna with a surprising bite of pleasure, to spread the news of our Samaritan-loving daughter. When she looked at Mary, her daughter was looking into her eyes.

"Mary," Anna began, "did you not think to bring the money home and ask Father or me what should be done?"

The little girl looked right at her. "Mother," she answered in her clear, serious voice, "If I had waited to ask you or Father, would we have found the family again?"

Joachim smiled in proud surprise at his daughter's wise answer, but Anna knew her child was not trying to be clever. "Well then, did you not think to ask your cousin, Elizabeth, who was there with you?"

A small frown shadowed the child's pretty face, and she turned to Elizabeth. "Cousin Elizabeth," she said, "I should have asked you. I'm sorry."

Elizabeth didn't know what to say. She kept gazing at Mary as though seeing the little girl for the first time. Mary turned back to Anna. "Mother, the woman had so many children. I could see they had not eaten; they even looked with hunger upon the herbs we'd gathered. All those children! And you and Father only have me, and I am never hungry. Was it wrong to give them the coin?"

Anna studied her beautiful, earnest child. Joachim opened his mouth as though to come to Mary's defense, but Anna raised her hand and he remained silent. She thought about reminding Mary of the separation between Jews and Samaritans, the enmity, but to what purpose? It would mean nothing to this daughter of hers whose hand was always open to give. Perhaps it should mean nothing to any of them. She considered telling Mary that a denarius was worth a great deal, and that her father worked hard for what they had and should have been consulted, but the girl was right about this as well: they had enough to eat, everything they needed.

Mary, Joachim, and Elizabeth all had their eyes fixed on Anna, as though waiting for her judgment. Still gazing at her daughter, she finally said, "No, child. It was not wrong to give them the coin. You did what the Lord would wish you to do." The only one of the three who didn't look relieved at Anna's judgment was Mary, and Anna knew why. There was something in her daughter that always knew what was right...and did it.

Now, years later, Mary had been watching her silently, patiently, as Anna remembered all these things. After a while Mary softly asked her again, "Mother, do you not believe me?"

Anna sighed and met her daughter's gaze. "I will speak to your father."

"I can tell him myself," Mary offered, but before she'd

even finished speaking, Anna declared, "No! That is the last thing that we need! I will tell him. Mary, think about it. Your father is not a young man. Think how this news will affect him."

For the first time, Anna saw a troubled look pass over Mary's calm features. Yet she knew it was not a look of guilt or shame; it was a look that said that Mary, for the first time perhaps, had realized how much harm her situation could do to those she loved. And she was sorry for it. Anna had no words to comfort or reassure her; better that she begin to understand what her life would be from now on.

"Go to eat tonight with one of your friends, maybe Sarah. Her father did well at the market yesterday, and they will have plenty. Leave your father and me to eat alone tonight. I will speak with him then."

She'd prepared Joachim's favorite meal and even given him some of the wine they kept for special meals. He had finished eating, and now Anna poured a little more wine for him. "Husband, I have something to tell you."

He laughed. "You mean now that you have fed me and given me wine, you are ready to tell me the reason for such lavish treatment!"

But when she did not smile or laugh in return, he grew somber. "What is it, Anna?"

"Hear me through all that I must say. It will be hard for you to bear, but I beg you to stay calm and hear me."

Twice during the telling, she'd had to grasp his hands to keep him from tearing out what little hair he had left. At least once the blood had suffused his face so utterly, she left off speaking until he could catch his breath and take some more wine. At length she was silent. The look on his face nearly broke her own heart. Though an old man, Joachim was strong, and raising his young daughter had kept him youthful. Now, in the course of a few minutes, he'd aged more than in the past thirteen perfect years with Mary, and she—the child who had kept him young and who loved him as only a daughter can love a doting father—was the cause. He believed that his daughter had betrayed and shamed him. Anna was glad that Mary was not here to see.

Joachim finally forced himself to raise his eyes to Anna. The disbelief and fury and shame had all passed away. The only thing left in him was a look of utter helplessness in the eyes that dully searched hers.

"How could she have done this? To us? To herself? *To Joseph?* Anna, he could have her stoned! Doesn't she understand this?"

"She believes she is doing God's will. That is all she considers to be important."

"God's will!" Joachim exploded. "Here is proof that she has lost her wits! How could it be God's will to shame herself and all of us this way? How could it be God's will to break the law he himself has given us through Moses? How could..."

Anna remained silent as his words drained away. He looked at her suspiciously. "Wife? Surely you don't believe this story she has made up to cover her shame?"

Anna still did not speak, but when she looked at him, his eyes widened in disbelief. "You do! You do believe this, this, foolishness! This…lie!"

Finally, she asked, "Has Mary ever lied to us?"

Joachim hardly paused. "That is not important. She is lying now. She must be!"

"Answer me, husband. Has she ever, once, lied to us or been false in any way?"

He drew breath to speak, but then said nothing. Anna secretly rejoiced to see a light return to his eyes, if only the light of contention. "How can you believe such a story?" he demanded. "Has anything like this been known from the beginning of time?"

Anna had her answer ready. "Why have you been so proud of teaching your daughter the prophets and the Scripture if you yourself do not believe them?"

His eyes widened. "*I! I*, not believe Scripture? I deny the prophets?"

Anna proclaimed: "'*Therefore, the Lord himself will give you a sign. Look, the virgin is with child and shall bear a son, and shall name him Immanuel*'" [Isaiah 7:14].

Joachim narrowed his eyes at her. For a long time, he did not speak. When he did, his voice was ragged, with hope and fear battling doubt and fear: "Could it be…Do you think…Mary? *Our child*?"

Anna knew this was the time to press her advantage. "She knew about Elizabeth. Days before we knew. She said the angel told her this as well."

They stared at each other for several minutes, this old and loving couple who had known so much sadness and so much joy together. At length, Anna asked, "What are we to do now?"

Joachim's strength had returned. "We need time to think about this. To pray and ask God's help. There is only one thing to do. We must send her away for now, south to the hill country. We must send her to Elizabeth and Zechariah."

PRAY

Saint Ann, you witnessed what you thought was the end of all your hopes and dreams, and yet God transformed your fear and anguish into a new beginning for the entire world! What you heard as disaster turned out to be the glorious fulfillment of all history. When my life leads me to a precipice or, more likely, a small crack in the path I've set for myself, help me to remember that by seeking God's will, I will always find my true way. Amen.

ACT

Think of an event in your past, large or small, when you felt that your plans had completely fallen through, that your careful preparations were for naught, and that the future looked dim, bleak, or uncertain. Now consider your reaction. Did you rail against fate, circumstances, or even God? Did you blame others or berate yourself? Or did you try to discern God's will in what had happened? If you could react all over again to this time or event, what would you do? What will you do when something like it happens in the future?

QUESTIONS

1. Have you ever encountered—in your own life or through friends and family members—a situation where parents have resisted God's will for their child? What is the parental motivation? Protection? Selfishness? Both?

2. Do our children belong to us? Or to God? How is that conflict, if it exists, manifested in Christian families today?

Two

MARY

In those days Mary set out and went with haste to a Judean town in the hill country, where she entered the house of Zechariah and greeted Elizabeth. When Elizabeth heard Mary's greeting, the child leaped in her womb. LUKE 1:39–41

THEY HAD ONLY TRAVELED A HALF-DAY'S JOURNEY FROM NAZARETH, AND ALREADY MARY MISSED HER PARENTS. She had never before been separated from them, not even for a night. Even when she had been betrothed to Joseph a few months ago, she had not been worried; she knew she would be in the same village as her parents, only a few minutes away. But now she was going to Elizabeth, and although she had made this trip several times with her parents, this was the first time she was going without them,

traveling with another family from Nazareth that had business in Jerusalem. Mary was to make the difficult five-day
journey with them, and they would leave her with Elizabeth
and Zechariah before they continued on to Jerusalem.
In return for the family agreeing to take her along, Mary
would help Lea, the mother, care for her two young children along the way.

Mary had agreed to this arrangement, and she was
especially looking forward to seeing Elizabeth and witness-
ing this other miraculous pregnancy with her own eyes, but
she was dismayed at her father's decree that she must leave
Nazareth immediately. Her beloved father, whose affection-
ate eyes had been always on her from the moment of her
birth, could not meet her gaze when he told her she was to
go to Elizabeth and Zechariah. It was his distress with her,
more than anything else, that had made her protest.

"Father," she'd said, "I do not wish to run away. I have
nothing to be ashamed of. I am doing what God wants of
me."

Joachim had been uncharacteristically abrupt with his
answer. "It is also God's will that you are still my child, and
your mother and I need time to understand what has happened. We need to think about Joseph, what to say to him,
what he might do. You don't seem to understand your...
your situation. We need to make a plan, Mary."

Mary had said, "God has a plan, Father. We can do no
more than to wait for its fulfillment."

Impatience, anger, and fear all flashed in Joachim's eyes.
He took a deep breath, turned away from her, and said,

"You will go to Elizabeth. We have made the arrangements. You leave tomorrow."

Later that night her parents had invited Joseph to their home so that Mary could take leave of her husband. Before he'd arrived, Anna had seated Mary in the shadows and carefully arranged her robe so as to cover the slight thickening that only Anna could see. Mary hardly knew her husband. Though they'd been betrothed for several months now, they'd spent little time together. Before the angel had come to her, she'd felt sad, even fearful, about being married to this quiet man who was much older than she, but her time with the angel had relieved her of all fear. Whatever role God had chosen for Joseph, Mary knew that he would play it. Even if he himself was not yet aware of it.

Joseph had seemed confused, not understanding the abrupt departure of his betrothed to spend an unsettled amount of time with a cousin nearly a hundred miles away. He was a man of little speech during the best of times, and this sudden announcement of her trip seemed to rob him of all words. It had been an uncomfortable evening for all of them. Joachim and Anna had tried feverishly to keep the conversation alive, talking about nothing and trying to avoid a moment where Joseph might question his wife's plan to go to the Judean hill country. Mary had said little, watching Joseph when she could do so without seeming bold, and feeling sorry for her parents. She could tell that Joseph knew something was wrong, but didn't know whether, or how, to ask about it. Her father was a man who loved words, but even he couldn't talk through the entire visit. Finally, as he was preparing to take leave of them, Joseph turned directly to Mary.

"You will return before our year's betrothal is complete?"

He made it a question rather than a command, and for that Mary was grateful. But before she could think how to answer, Joachim broke in with what they all recognized as false heartiness. "Of course she will! She is only going to her cousin to help until Elizabeth's baby comes." He laughed loudly. "Mary has been looking forward to the year's end so that she can leave her old parents behind and be in charge of her own household!"

Joseph looked alarmed at this answer, or perhaps it was the manner in which it was delivered. He looked steadily at Mary. She calmly met his gaze. "God willing, I will return in good time," she said. He had nodded once and left. Afterwards, her parents, unused to dissembling and falseness, had been exhausted, and this morning, when they had risen before dawn to see her off, they looked old and weary.

Mary could not help but worry about them as she journeyed south with Lea and her family. Since the angel had come, she'd thought about little besides his announcement and its fulfillment, but now she had time to consider what all of it would mean to the people she loved. Her parents were old, and she had seen them age rapidly over the last few days. This morning, when they had risen in the darkness to see her off, she had hardly recognized them. They looked worn and shaken; her mother's face was haggard, and her father was pale and silent. The angel hadn't talked about that. Would her part in God's plan hasten their deaths? Would they ever see the holy child to be born—of their own flesh and blood?

Such thoughts had never occurred to her before. She'd always been certain of her future. She would live with Joseph, close to her parents, and Anna would help her bear and raise her children. Such things were never in doubt for her before. But now? Now, she did not know what might happen in the next day, the next instant. This brief separation from her parents was forcing her to realize that there may be longer and deeper separations to come. From the moment the angel had left her, Mary had not doubted God's will for her and the child. Even now, she didn't question it, but what of Joachim and Anna? Did her parents deserve what was to come upon them?

There was not a moment in her thirteen years that she had not felt loved by them. Their love was her earliest memory, her first thought, the only thing she'd known, and the longest thing she'd known. The first thing she could remember hearing was her father's voice, singing to her, reading her Scripture, comforting her when she'd fallen or hurt herself in some small way. The first thing she could remember tasting was the choicest morsel from her mother's plate. The first thing she could remember seeing was her mother's face peering down at her with delight and curiosity. The first thing she could remember smelling was her mother's cooking, and the first thing she could remember feeling was the comfort and safety of her father's strong arms.

Not once had he made her feel that he would have

preferred a son, though a son was what all men wanted. Yet Joachim had always acted as though she were son and daughter for him, enough and more than enough. He had taught her Scripture as though she were the son of a rabbi. Often when she was just a small girl, he would sweep her away from her mother's cooking and mending lessons to take her on long walks through Nazareth, as proud to be seen walking and talking with his daughter as he would have been were she a son. He endured the teasing and laughter of the other villagers, convinced that he had the best of all worlds in her.

Before long he was proved right. As Mary grew older, the snickers of those who'd mocked his devotion to his daughter turned to grudging nods of approval and even envy. Never had there been such a girl, the kinder ones would exclaim. Never had there been a daughter so obedient to both her parents. Her goodness was extolled in the small and sometimes narrow-minded community of Nazareth. Though she laughed and smiled often, a harsh word never passed her lips and she was always ready to help or offer consolation. She seemed almost to anticipate her parents' wishes so that there were never demands of her, only requests that were met almost before they were uttered. From Anna she learned how to cook and weave and sew, and she had her mother's calm, constant nature. From Joachim she learned history and Scripture and how to recognize God's wisdom in the world around her. From one end of Nazareth to another, her virtues were spoken of, yet there were those whose admiration too often crossed the line into jealousy.

But why did they marvel? Mary wondered now as she held Lea's youngest child napping in her arms. *How could I have been otherwise with parents like mine? How could I do wrong when I was so completely loved? How could I be harsh or mean with others, when I never heard a harsh or mean word against me in my own home? The Lord blessed me with good parents; beyond that, I am not so very remarkable.*

Of course, by the time Mary was of age, many parents wanted her for their sons. But Joachim had turned down offer after offer of marriage from other families, only agreeing when Joseph came forward, the good and quiet Joseph.

"He will take care of you, Mary," Joachim had said to her months ago when telling her of Joseph's suit. "He has agreed to let you stay with us a little longer than usual only because he knows you are young and that I don't want to part with you soon. He is considerate, and he makes a good living. A carpenter can go anywhere in the world and find work."

"But, Father," she'd said a little anxiously, "where would I go? Surely Joseph won't want to leave Nazareth. Surely we'll settle in his house near you and Mother."

Joachim had smiled, secretly pleased at her wish to stay close to them. "Of course, of course, Mary, I am only saying that a good carpenter need never worry about his living. Joseph will always take good care of you and your children." Joachim had been so pleased to have chosen such a good husband. "He is the one who comes closest to deserving you, my daughter."

But what did her father think now? Mary thought that

her mother was slowly coming to believe her, but Joachim? Would he ever believe the words of the angel that she'd repeated to him? It was different for a father—she somehow knew this—when it came to a daughter. While Anna was concerned about the villagers and the consequences under the law, Joachim was simply hurt. He thought his beloved girl had become something unimaginable to him. He grieved as much for the loss of her, or who he had thought her to be, as he did for her reputation.

Mary felt a wave of sorrow at the thought of her father's disappointment. "Please, Lord," she prayed silently, "let him see. Let him believe. Let him know. Protect him from this pain."

Unconsciously her hand strayed from the tousled head of Lea's sleeping son to her own stomach. She felt the small swell beneath her hand and her sorrow receded. It was a wonder to her: almost from the moment the angel had stopped speaking, she had felt this child and been comforted. She knew from other women that they never felt their babies so early; she knew it was impossible for them. But for her, he had been there from the first instant. A warmth. A humming. A soft song that never left her and that, in moments like these, calmed her with a sense of peace no matter how her thoughts had worried her.

It is as though, Mary thought to herself, he is giving me life rather than me giving it to him.

"Mary," Lea said, noting Mary gently rubbing her stomach, "you've had no breakfast! You must be hungry. Here, let me take that lazy boy, and you have some bread."

Mary smiled. Lea was always talking about her two young sons as though they were the greatest burdens on earth, but everyone knew it was quite the opposite with her. Though it was Lea's way to complain about her sons, she was more than a little proud of them. Indeed, her complaints were a form of boasting, and Mary had noticed this in other mothers. She is mostly proud of having them, thought Mary, as though that alone had secured her place in the world. And in their world, it truly had. Since the angel, Mary had made a practice of studying the women in Nazareth with small children. There was a sense of self-satisfaction about them, a sense almost of relief. The main work of their lives was done. And if they'd borne sons, all the better. God had blessed them, and they knew it. No one could look upon them with pity or scorn, as Mary knew they had once looked upon her own mother.

For Lea, only five years older than Mary, having produced two healthy sons who'd survived their births was the most important thing she would do. She had proved herself. And if she had more sons, and even a daughter or two, her power and contentment would only grow. Already, her sons had elevated her in their world, and, mistaking Mary's silent study of the young boys for yearning, Lea gave her a pitying, superior look. "Don't worry," Lea said, squeezing Mary's arm, "soon you will have your own healthy son to present to Joseph."

Sooner than you think, thought Mary, and she tried not to laugh.

Yet, she was coming to understand Lea's pride. Five years

ago, Lea had been nothing more than a young girl about to enter her husband's house. She didn't know God's will for her, as Mary did. Lea hadn't known whether God would bless her, or how long it might take, or whether she would suffer childlessness. She was like so many other young women from Nazareth and every other place in Israel and Judah who didn't know if they would live with the shame of not producing a son, or any child at all. They didn't know if their husbands would reject them, send them back to their parents, or even take other wives. They lived in that kind of fear and uncertainty from the moment of their betrothals.

Though God had given Mary a different kind of life with its own challenges, she would never know the kind of uncertainty that made Lea exult in her sons while others waited in fearful prayer for the children that would win them acceptance in the eyes of their world. God had given Mary knowledge of the blessed child growing in her. He had spared her the fear of being thought barren, useless. She knew she would bear a son, though who he was, who he would be, was something she could only imagine. Nothing that the prophets had said of her son could prepare her, she knew that. She could only trust to God and the son within her, filling her with this calming song and giving her courage.

It happened on the last day of their journey.
They were rising at dawn and preparing to set out, when Mary noticed Lea staring at her. Mary's hand rested, as it

so often did these days, upon her stomach. Lea's eyes narrowed. She grasped Mary's arm and pulled her aside from her husband and children.

"I cannot believe Joseph has done this!" She hissed. "You should not have let him, Mary. You, of all women, were thought to be virtuous! You know you were to wait! It is the law!"

Without thinking, Mary uttered, "But Joseph did not…"

Her voice trailed off as she saw the look of righteous indignation on Lea's face harden into something horrified and then harshly forbidding. Lea released Mary's arm as though it had burned her hand and stepped back. Mary started to speak, to explain, but when Lea raised her hand for silence, Mary knew there was no appealing to her. Lea's face closed and when she finally spoke, her voice was cold and low, and she did not once look at Mary.

"If it were not the last day, if we were not hours away from your cousin's, I would leave you here on the road. As it is, for the sake of your poor parents, I will say nothing to my husband and we will bring you to Zechariah and Elizabeth. Do not speak to me. Do not touch my children. Do not eat our bread. You will walk behind the donkey and the cart."

With a final look of disgust Lea backed away and did not speak to or even look at Mary again. Mary walked in silence for the two hours it took to reach Elizabeth's village. Her heart pounded in her chest. No one had ever spoken to her like this in all her life. No one had ever stared at her so disdainfully. No one had ever expressed such hateful rejection. And now she knew what her parents had worried about; now she felt it. Her ears felt on fire with Lea's words, and her eyes stung with the memory of Lea's face. Her hands shook as she carried her belongings for the first time in the journey without anyone to help her. Though she knew she had no reason to feel ashamed, she did feel the shame of this treatment, and she understood it might be like this from now on. It was not only that no one would believe her; it was that no one would even listen to her; no one would even want to be near her.

And Joseph? For the first time she fully realized what he would face. If she tried to defend him by telling the truth, as she had with Lea, she would not be believed and he would be nothing more than an object of pity. If she said nothing, people would think that he had broken their law and his vow to her parents by knowing her as wife before the time of betrothal was finished. He, too, would be despised and rejected.

She avoided the confused glances of Lea's husband, and once, when the youngest boy reached out to Mary, who'd become his favorite, she turned away when Lea roughly snatched him back. When they reached the outskirts of Elizabeth's village, Lea said loudly to her husband, "Mary wishes to walk the rest of the way so she can surprise her cousin. We need go no farther with her." Without any other leave-taking, they kept going. Before they disappeared along the road to Jerusalem, Mary saw Lea speaking to her husband with many gestures. She knew that her parents would have no chance to make the plan they so desperately hoped for; by sunset on the day Lea returned to Nazareth, everyone would know. Including Joseph.

Mary breathed deeply and placed both hands gently on the place where the child was. Her heart slowed its wild beating. The child's song remained, but she knew now that other sounds, angry and hurtful, would surround her as well. All they had, she and her son, was each other and God.

Mary saw Elizabeth first. Mary paused, just out of sight, observing Elizabeth as she used palm branches to sweep around the house where she and Zechariah lived. Her older cousin looked radiant; that she bore a child was clear, even beneath her voluminous robes. She could hear Elizabeth singing a hymn as she worked. Joachim and Anna had had no time to send Elizabeth word that their daughter was coming to her, or in what state. Mary hesitated. Would Elizabeth, who now carried her own miracle son, condemn her, too? Mary was not sure how she would bear it—or what she would do—if Elizabeth and Zechariah did not believe her. Still, there was time yet to tell them; her son was not yet obvious to the world. Lea would have never seen had not Mary been careless. She stepped forward.

Without even looking up, Elizabeth paused. She gasped and bent a little before straightening to look searchingly into Mary's face. Elizabeth's entire being was alight with such joy that Mary felt tears come into her own eyes.

36

Elizabeth took Mary into her arms, crying, *"Blessed are you among women, and blessed is the fruit of your womb. And why has this happened to me that the mother of my Lord comes to me? And blessed is she who believed that there would be a fulfillment of what was spoken to her by the Lord"* [Luke 1:42–43, 45].

And finally, Mary wept.

PRAY

Mother of God, as I try to prepare for your son's birthday, I find myself besieged from all sides with pressures and irritations that drain away my joyful anticipation. There's a virus going around at work, and I'm terrified I'll get it. I have dozens of cookies to bake, and a dish to prepare for the church potluck. My boss has announced there will be no bonuses this year, so there goes the money I'd counted on for presents. I don't know what to get anyone, anyway. My friends don't have time to talk, or even to text, and, the truth is, I don't have time for them. The weather is miserable, and my spirit is even bleaker. Mary, help me to remember that your path to the first Christmas was more difficult and complicated than anything I can even imagine. Be with me as I struggle to open myself to the true spirit of this blessed time of waiting. Show me what is important. Guide me to people who will love me for who I am and not judge me for what I cannot get done. Help me to make the celebration of your son my Christmas priority. Amen.

ACT

Find time today to spend five minutes in a church. (Yes, you do have five minutes.) It doesn't have to be your church. It can be a church you pass by regularly and are curious about. It can be a church you've never seen before. It can be a church in another town or city. If the church is open, go in and sit quietly—near the manger if one is set up. If the church is not open and the weather is amenable, sit on the steps or nearby; if the weather is not good, simply sit in your car near the church. Close your eyes. Breathe deeply. Spend five precious minutes with the Lord and his mother. Remind yourself that this is what Christmas is all about.

QUESTIONS

1. If God asked you to bear or raise his Son, what would your response be?

2. How does the church, in its teachings about and relationship with Mary, fully take into account her humanity?

Three

ELIZABETH
& ZECHARIAH

Then his father Zechariah was filled with the Holy
Spirit and spoke this prophecy: "Blessed be the Lord
God of Israel, for he has looked favorably on his people
and redeemed them. He has raised up a mighty savior
for us in the house of his servant David, as he spoke
through the mouth of his holy prophets from of old."

Luke 1:67–70

ZECHARIAH WAS COMPLETELY STILL. He gazed upon the
three of them, lying close together for warmth—his wife,
Elizabeth, and their young cousin Mary, with his precious
son, John, between them, kicking his legs a little, with his
eyes wide open. The two women, so different in age and
demeanor, had grown quite close over the past months,
and on this, Mary's last night with them, she, Elizabeth,
and the baby had laid down together for warmth and

comfort. They would miss Mary more than they had ever imagined. Zechariah smiled at John, who seemed to be staring back solemnly at his father, his eyes lit with curiosity. Of course, Zechariah told himself, the infant was too small to even know what he was seeing, but still—there was something already about his son that made him different from other babies.

What will you become? Who will you be? Zechariah wondered, watching John, who was curled up happily between the womb that had borne him and the womb bearing the One he would serve. From the moment Gabriel had struck him dumb in the temple nearly a year ago, Zechariah had never again doubted God's goodness or his plan. And from the moment God had freed him from silence, he had been praising that very plan. But now, staring down at his child who had been born, and the One to be born, the living fulfillment of God's plan, Zechariah could not help but be a little afraid. All of history had led to this scene in front of him, and all of history would turn on what happened next. In this moment of pure peace, he wondered what would become of them, John and the One growing inside Mary.

It was one thing to know about that history, to have read the prophets, to know God's covenant with Abraham, renewed again with Moses and David, to have spent a lifetime studying and debating these words. It was one thing to yearn for the Messiah and his herald, to wait and search and pray for their coming. It was quite another thing, thought Zechariah wryly, to be the father of one and the cousin of the other. It was quite another thing to see them both, just a handsbreadth apart, perhaps in the last moment of peace and silence they would have together.

The prophecies didn't say what would happen to the one who would go before the Messiah, did they? Zechariah thought to himself. *All this time I've waited and prayed for this herald of God, and now that I find him to be my own son, I realize that I never considered how he would be an infant and a boy and a man, a real person with a real life. But what sort of a life? Suddenly, I am not a priest or a student and debater of Scripture, but a father filled with pride and fear for his son. And instead of my mind being filled with unadulterated joy for the fulfillment of God's plan, all I can think of is what will it mean for him? How will I protect him? Will he suffer? Will his life be difficult? Or will he be heard and received by the greatest in our nation? Will he live in fine rooms and sleep in chambers set aside for him by kings and Pharisees?*

But before any of that can happen, will I be a good father to him? What must I teach him? What will he already know from God and God's angels? Will I see the fulfillment of the prophecies in his very nature? And when? When will the day come when I will recognize him as the greatest prophet God has created? What if I fail? What if I cannot teach him? How can I father such a one as Gabriel said he would be?

And what of Mary and her Son, the Blessed One, the Messiah? Seeing the girl here in front of me, I am forced to acknowledge that he, too, will be a little boy, younger even than my John. He, too, will be subject to parents and teach-

ers. How can this be? How can anyone understand or live with this idea that God's own Messiah will be a helpless infant?

Zechariah recalled his argument with Elizabeth about Mary earlier in the day. "I don't think she should go back tomorrow," he'd declared stubbornly, repeating what he'd said three days ago when Mary had announced it was time for her to return to Nazareth. He had said nothing to Mary at the time, but as soon as he and Elizabeth were alone, he'd voiced his concerns. Today, they'd gone over the same points.

"She is determined to go," Elizabeth had answered him, "as you well know! We've talked to her about this, and she has not changed her mind."

"But do you agree?" he'd persisted. "Do you think she *should* go?"

"Husband, it doesn't matter what I think! Or what you think, for that matter. Don't you know I would love for her to stay? She has been nothing but a delight and a help to me since the day she came. Why would I not want to keep her near us?" Elizabeth was frustrated. "Do you think I want to send her back, given what is waiting for her there?"

"Have we any word at all from Anna and Joachim?"

"None," Elizabeth said, adding, "but the news cannot be good. The woman Mary traveled here with has long since returned to Nazareth, and Mary is convinced that she would have wasted no time telling everyone that Mary is pregnant."

"Then how can we send her back?" Zechariah asked ur-

gently. "We know the child she carries. Is it not our role—
my role—to protect her and the child? How do we know
she won't be stoned in Nazareth?"

"She says she knows that God will protect her," Elizabeth
said. "How can we argue with that? She carries God's Son!"

"That is the very thing!" Zechariah cried. "What if God
sent her to us for that very purpose, so that we would be
the ones to protect and shelter her and the child?"

"We don't know what God wills for his Son; we can
hardly know what God wills for our own son!" Elizabeth
answered. "We cannot stop her from returning, Zechariah;
you must accept this. She is worried about her parents and
wants to be with Anna for the birth. There is nothing we
can do."

He knew she was right. He'd already appealed to Mary a
number of times, but she had only smiled gently at him and
said, "It is time, Zechariah. I must go home."

As Zechariah watched, Mary's hand moved to her now
round belly, and John reached out with his tiny fist and
grasped her finger. In her sleep Mary smiled. Tears started
to his eyes as Zechariah remembered the day three
months ago that the weary and dismayed girl had walked
into their yard.

*He had been praying—though silently, since
the angel had taken his voice—with some
other men from the village when the boy that
Elizabeth had sent for him burst into the house.*

Another of the men chastised the child, but Zechariah could see the urgency in the boy's expression, and, worried that something had happened to his pregnant wife, he quickly followed him home. If the angel who called himself Gabriel had not taken his voice, the sight awaiting Zechariah would have left him speechless. He hurried into his house to find Elizabeth seated by their young cousin Mary, and his wife's arms were around the girl, comforting her.

Elizabeth looked up at him when he walked into the house and, as was her way, spoke directly, "Joachim and Anna have sent her to us. She carries the Messiah."

Zechariah had stepped back in disbelief, almost as if to defend himself against the onslaught of emotions that rose up at these words. "How could this be?" he might have said, if he could have spoken, or "What are you saying?" But as these words came into his mind, he remembered the reason he couldn't speak: his disbelief in the miracle the angel had announced to him months ago. Zechariah drew in a long breath. Would he now refuse to believe another miracle? The very miracle that would confirm the angel's words about the son he and Elizabeth awaited? He recalled Gabriel's words about their son, John: *"many will rejoice at his birth, for he will be great in the sight of the Lord...He will turn many of the people of Israel to the Lord their God. With the spirit and power of Elijah, he will go before him, to turn the hearts of parents to their children, and the disobedient to the wisdom of the righteous, to make ready a people prepared for the Lord"* [Luke 1:14–17].

His breathing ragged, Zechariah stared at the two women. He tried to force the words out of his mind, but they kept returning. How could this be? Could it be that the Lord God intended for John's cousin to be the Christ, the One he would prepare the world to know? I am an old man, thought Zechariah. How am I to understand such things? How am I to cope with all this?

Elizabeth's gaze had stayed upon him, but now, for the first time, Mary raised her face to his. He could see that she had been weeping, but already the comfort of being with Elizabeth and seeing the angel's words fulfilled in her pregnancy had restored Mary's courage. This girl, hardly known to him except as a sweet child with whom God had blessed Anna and Joachim in their old age, now looked at him with eyes that seemed to plumb the depth of his soul, eyes filled with understanding and compassion and certainty. Into the profound silence of that moment, Elizabeth spoke again. "Zechariah. Husband. When she came into the yard, your son leapt in my womb and the Holy Spirit made me a prophet. Her Son is the Blessed One."

And as Zechariah was released from his paralysis of mind, the other words about John spoken by Gabriel rushed into his memory: "*even before his birth, he will be filled with the Holy Spirit*" [Luke 1:15].

They might have been in awe of Mary from that moment forward, but the girl herself strove against this. She was everywhere, helping, and often had to be told to rest, or she might have been mistaken for a new servant. She assumed many of the household duties as Elizabeth progressed in her days of confinement, and it was clear that she was the obedient daughter of older parents. She knew how to meet their needs and provide for their small comforts without asking. The weight and magnificence of the knowledge they shared drew them closer together, and though Elizabeth and Zechariah were leaders in their village, they began to rely more on Mary to be their community. The enormity of what they knew together made it difficult to spend time in the company of others. Fortunately, their friends and neighbors thought nothing strange in this, believing it natural that a woman of Elizabeth's age should spend these months apart with a young relative. Indeed, the village elders were secretly relieved to see less of Zechariah; the silence that God had imposed upon him discomfited them, nor had he communicated its meaning to them. And in both their hearts, Elizabeth and Zechariah were silently grateful that Mary would be with Elizabeth at John's birth, for they felt certain that God would bless the birth if the mother of his Son was present and assisting.

When she wasn't making herself useful to them, Mary spent a good deal of time talking quietly with Elizabeth; and later, as he grew more accustomed to the magnitude of what her presence represented, Zechariah joined them. Somehow his silence had become less of a hindrance since Mary's arrival. She and Elizabeth seemed to understand him without speech; he needed to write only a few words on the tablet he used to communicate for them to know his thoughts. The three spent many evenings after supper reading the psalms and the prophets, trying to understand what God might want of them in the coming days. These discussions had only intensified in the past few days since God had given Zechariah back his voice so that he could lift it in prophecy and praise after John's birth.

Some passages from sacred Scripture encouraged them, confirming what they'd already experienced. Yes, the Messiah would be from the House of David, for so was Mary, and if by some miracle Joseph kept her as wife, so was he. Yes, he would be called by God from Nazareth, for that is where he was conceived. Yes, he would be born of the virgin to a people desperate for redemption and freedom from their oppressors. But some of the familiar prophecies they now studied with a new and more discerning eye confused them.

"How is it that he will be called out of Egypt?" Elizabeth had puzzled that night of John's naming. "We are not in Egypt. Thank the Lord! Is the prophet talking about Abraham or Moses and not the Messiah?"

"He may be talking of all three," Zechariah said, shrugging. "After all, any descendant of Abraham or Moses could be said to be called out of Egypt. Mary's child need not set foot out of Galilee or Judah and the people could still say he was 'called out of Egypt.'"

"But do you think that John must go to *Egypt* ahead of him?" Elizabeth worried, gazing over at her sleeping infant. "How are we to manage that? Are we to leave here and raise him away from our people?"

There seemed to be no clear answers to these questions,

and yet, they could not help but ask. One reason Zechariah didn't want Mary to return to Nazareth was what the prophet had declared about the Messiah coming from Bethlehem.

"Look," he'd said to her the day after she announced she would return to Nazareth, "the prophet tells us plainly, '*And you, Bethlehem, in the land of Judah, are by no means least among the rulers of Judah; for from you shall come a ruler who is to shepherd my people Israel*' [Micah 5:2]. Mary, what else can that mean but that your son must be born in Bethlehem? And isn't that why God put it into your father's heart to send you to us? We can protect you here. Who knows what awaits you in Nazareth? Joseph may have already passed judgment based on Lea's accusation. Remain here with us; we are only a few miles from Bethlehem, and we can take lodgings there when your time comes to fulfill Scripture. We can return here afterward, and your parents can come to us if they wish. Shouldn't John and your son be raised together? Nazareth is five days of hard travel away! Why would God will you to return there with the child growing in you for over six months now? It makes no sense!"

Mary had laughed. "How can we know what makes sense to God, cousin? If we try to understand any of this by human ways, we can only fail. Who can know what God will do now? Can we know the power of the mind of God? Does God need our permission or help to accomplish his will? We can only hope to follow where he leads, and now I know he leads me back to the parents I promised I would return to. I have never yet lied to them, and I must not start now."

There had been no appealing to her on the subject. But while Mary did not trouble herself with trying to discover how to accomplish God's will, both Elizabeth and Zechariah had noticed that she studied often the Scriptures describing the Messiah, what he would be like, and most of all, how he would suffer. "What kind of man will he be," she asked them, "who will have all authority and be a warrior with a mouth like a sharp sword, and yet will not break a bruised reed or quench a faltering wick or raise his voice?"

Elizabeth had no answer, nor did Zechariah find a way to comfort her when she murmured, "How is it that after God lifts him up, according to the prophet, God will then cast him down? For in almost the same breath, Isaiah says, '*He was despised and rejected by others, a man of suffering and acquainted with infirmity; and as one from whom others hide their faces, he was despised. Surely he has borne our infirmities and carried our diseases, yet we accounted him stricken, struck down by God and afflicted*'"[Isaiah 53:3–4).

Mary paused and looked searchingly at Zechariah. She whispered, "Am I to bear God's Son so that the Lord God can make him suffer and die?"

Neither Zechariah nor Elizabeth knew how to answer, for they all knew that the rest of Isaiah's prophecy was even more distressing: *he was oppressed and he was afflicted, yet he did not open his mouth; like a lamb that is led to the slaughter, and like a sheep that before its shearers is silent, so he did not open his mouth. By a perversion of justice, he was taken away. Who could have imagined his future*? (Isaiah: 53:7–8). And they couldn't—and suddenly they weren't sure they wanted to—answer. Elizabeth found herself stealing a glance at John, who rested against her, and she held him closer. Suddenly, whether Mary's son was born in Nazareth or Bethlehem or even Egypt did not seem so important.

Now that it was time for Mary to leave, Zechariah did not want to waken the sleeping women with John warm and content between them. The sun would soon rise and the caravan with which they had arranged for Mary's return journey would soon arrive. He told himself that they would certainly see her again; surely the Lord would want her son to be acquainted with his servant, John? Zechariah's hands trembled as he clasped them in prayer for Mary, for her son, and for Elizabeth and their son, John. Then, he drew a steady breath and rose to wake them.

PRAY

Saints Elizabeth and Zechariah, how I would love to hear God's words and instructions the way you did! How I would love for God to tell me what he wants from me, to instruct me clearly and precisely through an angel! I wonder what it must have felt like for you to know God's will directly! And then, I wonder: could I handle it? Could I handle it if God were to speak to me or through me directly? Could I willingly pay the price you paid for such direct communication? Could I give up all worldly concerns, stop worrying about what people think of me, trust completely to God's will and do nothing to protect myself against the scorn, curiosity, and sanctions of others? Could I give up my child to do God's will if it meant losing her or him? When I think about you both and how you gave yourselves and your son to God's word and will, I pray not only that I come to understand God's will for me, but that I have the faith and courage to follow and fulfill it. Amen.

ACT

Live today as if God has instructed you about what to do to follow his will…because he has! Every teaching from Jesus in the gospels comes from God, and some of them are repeated frequently. If you want to know what God wants you to do, read what Jesus said. Today, be a good neighbor and help someone in trouble. Today, feed the hungry, clothe the naked, visit the sick or imprisoned. Today, give your money to the poor, without judging them or wondering if they're worthy of your contribution. Today, willingly pay your taxes. Today, be as quiet as possible, saying little beyond yes or no. Today, forgive another. Today, realize that you know what God wants from you; all you have to do is do it.

QUESTIONS

1. Have you ever found yourself in a situation where you simply couldn't know—from Scripture or from prayer—what God wanted you to do? How do you navigate such a situation?

2. How are we to react to personal or communal dilemmas/questions when Scripture, prayer, and even religious teachings seem to suggest different resolutions—or even contradict each other?

Four

JOSEPH

Her husband Joseph, being a righteous man and
unwilling to expose her to public disgrace, planned to
dismiss her quietly. But just when he had resolved to do
this, an angel of the Lord appeared to him in a dream
and said, "Joseph, son of David, do not be afraid to take
Mary as your wife, for the child conceived in her is from
the Holy Spirit." MATTHEW 1:19–20

WHAT JOSEPH HOPED MOST OF ALL WAS THAT SHE
WOULDN'T COME BACK. For so long, the greatest desire of
his heart was to make Mary his wife, to live with her and
comfort her and love her and receive some small measure
of all that back from her, and now the best he could hope
for was to never see her again.

He prayed for this every day and every night.

When Lea first returned nearly three months ago from
her journey to Jerusalem, he had refused to believe what

she said about Mary. Not that she told him directly. No, she made sure every woman in Nazareth knew, but she did not come to him. By the time she sent her wretched husband to give him the news, it was no longer news. By then Joseph had been anticipating his visit, and had sent the cringing young man away almost before he'd finished mumbling his condemnation of Mary.

Until then, Joseph had not listened to the others; he couldn't. He'd told himself over and over that it couldn't be true. It was malicious gossip, started by Lea who had never been as popular or as pretty or certainly not as good as Mary. Mary simply wouldn't betray him that way. She wouldn't betray *herself* that way and definitely not her parents who rightly considered her the very light of their lives. More than any girl in Nazareth, Mary knew the law; Joachim had broken with tradition to teach his daughter the sacred Scriptures as he would have a son. Mary would not put her life and her soul at risk in such a way.

For some days Joseph had continued in his daily life, working, eating, sleeping, praying, and most of all, ignoring the pitying looks and sidelong glances that were sent in his direction. He held his head high and met the eyes of no man.

But he had not been able to stop the doubts in his mind. Why had Mary so abruptly agreed to the long, difficult journey south to Elizabeth and Zechariah? The trip was almost as long as the one from here to his own place of birth, Bethlehem. He'd wondered at the time why she'd made such a sudden decision, and now the question rose up like an ugly specter from the back of his thoughts. And why hadn't Joachim come to see him since Lea had returned? Why wasn't Joachim, his betrothed's father, here, rushing to defend her and deny Lea's malevolent story? Lea had been home and talking constantly for days now, yet there was no sign of Anna or Joachim.

Still, Joseph had bent his head over his worktable and tried to focus on nothing but his carpentry. Mary would be home soon, and in a few months his wife would come to live with him. He stubbornly clung to this and attempted to close his mind to any other thoughts.

And then Lea's husband had come to him and made his stuttering, shamefaced accusation. But even while coldly dismissing him, Joseph knew it was over. The pretense he had been grimly fixing in his mind of a contented, peaceful life with the purest, kindest girl in Nazareth was just that— a falsehood. He might have been able to continue to deny Mary's guilt even after Lea's husband came, except that the man used Mary's own words to condemn her. The man had told Joseph, "When Lea chastised her for being with you before the end of the betrothal, Mary had answered, 'But Joseph did not...'"

And as he watched the man scurry away, Joseph, God help him, could just hear her saying it.

No, he told himself, trying to summon up anger against his wife, *Joseph did not*! But even as he heard her words echo in his mind, he understood that in the very moment when Mary should have been worrying about herself— with her reputation, her life itself, at stake—she had tried to protect him. Almost from that first moment, whatever anger he wanted to, *longed* to, feel became sorrow and a searing disappointment unlike any he'd imagined. He felt most keenly a sense of his loss, and though he knew that it was Mary who could lose so much more, including her life, he did not feel the anger that might have freed him from his pain.

That night he had gone to Joachim and Anna. The shutters were drawn and the door was closed, but he steeled himself and went in. One look at them told him that any shred of hope he'd held was gone. They didn't say a word. Joachim could not even lift his face to meet Joseph's eyes, and the older man had aged a decade in the past few weeks. He was pale and seemed weary well beyond his advanced years. He'd risen heavily to his feet when Joseph first walked in, but after a swift glance up at him, Joachim lowered himself back into the chair where he'd been sitting in the shadows. Anna, though she looked spent and haggard, seemed stronger than her husband. She did not speak a word of denial, but gazed steadily at Joseph and did not seem as defeated as her husband. Though the light of humor and life had dimmed in Joachim's eyes, Anna's seemed to glow with intensity.

After a painful moment, Joseph broke the looming silence. "So it is true. You knew. You knew before she left."

Joachim seemed to reach into the depths of himself to summon the energy to answer. "It is why we sent her away. To gain time. To try to plan."

Joseph raised his voice in astonishment. "To gain time?

For what? Did you think I might grow blind over the next few months? Or that God might strike out the eyes of everyone in Nazareth so that they wouldn't see her shame? My shame? And plan? What plan could there be for this? What could you hope to do?"

Joachim slumped back as though Joseph had struck him, and despite himself, Joseph felt a surge of pity.

He asked more quietly, "Was she attacked? Taken by force?"

But before Joachim could answer, Anna moved toward Joseph and grasped his hand. It was all he could do not to pull it away, but she saw his aversion and held on more tightly.

"No man has touched her. She says that an angel came to her and told her that the child is the Son of God, the Son of David. The Messiah to come."

Joseph snatched his hand away and staggered back. He felt his breath leave him. Had Anna been driven out of her senses by the shame Mary had brought upon them? Had Mary herself lost all sense? Joseph looked at Joachim, who glanced up at him, briefly and with a small spark of hope, but then looked away again after observing Joseph's shock. "Anna," Joachim cautioned his wife in a low voice, "don't trouble him with that. How is he to believe this thing?"

But Anna had recaptured his hand, and when he now tried to pull away again, she stepped closer to him. "Joseph," she said urgently, "I believe my daughter."

Joseph managed to pry her hot fingers off his hand and move away. "What are you saying?" he whispered, his voice raw. "How can you believe…why do you?…is it not bad enough that she has betrayed me, but now you want me to believe—*everyone* to believe—that this is God's work? That an angel of God said this?"

"Not everyone, no, not everyone. But you! Yes! You, Joseph, you must believe." Anna was insistent. "Doesn't the prophet say that the virgin will be with child as a sign to all? Doesn't he say that the Messiah will be of the House of David—and you and Mary are both of David's line! Who is to say that Mary's son, whom you will raise, is not the fulfillment of the prophecy? Who is to say that this is not God's plan?"

Joseph thought he could not bear this. "This is madness! How can you utter these things before man or God, Anna? The prophet? Because of a few ancient lines among all the writings of Isaiah, you believe this? These prophecies are hundreds of years old, and has there been any sign of the Messiah? We have lived under Assyria and Babylon and we are now under the boot of Rome, and you think now God sends the Messiah? *Through Mary?* A girl living in *Nazareth?*"

Joseph shook his head in amazement and pity. He feared for them, for Mary, for all of them if this became known in the village. Such claims would only compound Mary's shame. He wanted nothing more now than to leave, to escape the madness of these two old people who, he now realized, had been more damaged by all of this than even he. Not knowing what else to say or how to protect them, he turned to the door, but Anna remained undaunted.

"My cousin Elizabeth who was known to be barren and is older than I was when I bore Mary, has conceived at the word of an angel. It is a miracle! And why do you think God gave Joachim and me Mary at our advanced age when I too was thought to be barren? Joseph, can you truly not see God's hand in all this?"

His compassion prevented him from answering. His head ached with pain and sadness as he said softly, "I must go."

As he reached the door, Anna spoke again and there was real fear in her voice. "Joseph, can you not try to believe her? Because if you cannot believe, what will become of her?"

He stopped. With his back to her parents, he breathed deeply. This, at least, was something he could do for them, something to spare them the ultimate grief. After this, he would be finished; he could walk away knowing he had done his best though the cost to him might be great. Slowly, he turned back to them.

"Do not worry for her life," he said gently. "I will not condemn her. I will make it known that I've decided to divorce her peaceably. There will be no trial or accusation. She will not be able to marry again, but..."

Joachim gave a sad, bitter smile. "But who would marry her anyway? It is true, and we thank you for your kindness, Joseph. It is more than we could rightly ask for." Anna made a gesture as if she would speak but Joachim, recovering his dignity for at least these few moments, motioned for her silence. He stood and, for the first time since Joseph had entered the house, looked directly at the younger man. "You are a good man. You would have made a fine husband. Thank you."

That had been three months ago, and Joseph had hoped that every day would get easier for him, but nothing of the sort had happened. Instead, each day he was more wracked with sorrow and dismay. Although, according to Lea's words, Mary had committed an unpardonable sin and done him a great wrong, he couldn't stop thinking about her. If someone had asked him, among all the women he had known, to name the one who would be least likely to fall to such a state, he would have named Mary. That was one of the reasons he'd chosen her to begin with: there was a purity in her that seemed to go far deeper than her body. She had a serenity, a calmness of spirit, a peace about her, that had convinced him that she would complete his life in a way he could not imagine without her. And that is what haunted him now: what would his life be without her?

But another thought troubled him as well—one that made no sense, one that lodged in his mind no matter how hard he tried to banish it. If someone had asked him, among all the women he had known, to name the one that he would consider most fitted to fulfilling the prophet's words, he would have named Mary.

But, no! This was the thinking of someone who had lost his wits! He had to stop. He had to find a way to think about his life without her. As time had passed, he'd been given fewer pitying glances, and the mocking looks he was sure followed him when his back was turned diminished as well. To avoid the talk and humiliating stares, Anna and Joachim seldom left their house, and Joseph had taken to leaving them water and food because he feared they would fall ill in their seclusion. Like most people in Nazareth, he wondered if they would leave, perhaps join Mary in the south. Whether they would or not became less interesting as time went on. To Lea's dismay, as long as Mary stayed away and her parents secluded themselves, Nazarene interest in the scandal waned. The excitement was over. In the daily struggle just to live, people were forgetting Mary.

But he couldn't forget her. Even as he prayed for her to stay away forever, he wondered in his heart whether he would ever see her again. And God answered the prayer of his heart.

He heard the silence first.

It was as though the entire village had paused in all its business, as if everyone had frozen in place making no sound, barely breathing. Joseph was working outside and the sudden change made him look up. Mary was at the edge of the village, taking leave of the people who had brought her home. Joseph waited for her to turn toward him, toward the many pairs of eyes fixed upon her. When she did, it was all he could do to keep from groaning. The child was visible in her. Even as the gasps and exclamations of the others filled the air, he silently mocked himself. *What did you expect*? *That Lea's words weren't true*? *That it was*

some nightmare that you would awaken from when she re-
turned, slim and pure and ready to prove them all liars and
gossips? You fool!

He knew that as soon as the others could tear their eyes
from her figure, slowly making its way toward her parents'
house, they would turn to him. They wanted to see his reaction. Some hoped to see his hatred, his fury. Word had long
since made it around Nazareth that he would privately divorce her, but now they would want to know if the sight of
her—the public shaming of him—would cause him to erupt
into a rage and change his mind. Without waiting for her
to pass close enough to speak, he hurried into his house.
Like a child, he hunched down in the one corner where he
couldn't be seen through the open windows and huddled
there until he heard the murmurings fade and knew that
she had entered her parents' house. It was only then that he
realized that he'd stopped breathing.

Why, *why* hadn't she stayed away? Why hadn't she spared
all of them—herself, her parents, and him—this slashed
opening of a wound that could never heal in her presence?
How had the goodness that he still believed was in her
permitted this? He could almost call it an act of cruelty...if
it had been anyone but Mary who'd committed it.

He was sitting over his uneaten dinner later that night
when she called out softly to him from the doorway. At
the sound of her voice, he started out of the chair and had
to hold himself back from running from the house, fleeing
past her into the night where she couldn't find him. *Joseph,*
he asked himself sternly, *are you not a man?*

Without turning to her, he said quietly, "Mary, please. Go away. You should not be here."

He heard the smile in her voice when she answered. "Why? Will our neighbors find a way to think even less of me? Should I be concerned about preserving my reputation in Nazareth?"

He felt anger stir, and he turned to her as she slipped into the room. "You joke? You think this is amusing, the hurt and pain you've caused? You have no concern for your reputation, and so you can smile, but what about mine? What about your parents, cowering in that house? How can you, Mary?"

Immediately she became serious. "Joseph, I'm sorry. I didn't intend to make light of this. But, please, you must try to understand. I cannot be sorry for doing God's will. I know the son I carry is from God. I know this, not only because the angel told me, but I know it now in my very bones, my deepest self. I have great comfort and, yes, joy in this. I cannot mourn and act ashamed when I am doing what God has asked of me."

Joseph could not look at her. She was glowing, her eyes alit in the darkness of the room. The girlish prettiness was gone, replaced by something deeper and more beautiful. He turned away. "What do you want?" he murmured.

"To thank you," she said simply. "You have acted merci-fully toward me and my parents. They've told me of your decision to not publicly condemn or accuse me, and of how you've brought them food and water in these past months. You are a good man, Joseph, and I wanted you to know that

I understand the depth of your kindness."

Joseph couldn't help himself. He groaned. "Mary, why did you come back?"

She looked at him silently for a long moment. "Because it was time."

She turned to go, but when she reached the door, she paused. Without facing him she said quietly, "Joseph, I shall be sorry if I must lose you as my husband."

For the first time he heard true sadness in her voice. Then she was gone. Joseph dropped his head into his hands.

There was anger and agitation in Nazareth when the news came from Rome that the emperor had commanded all in Rome's occupied lands to be registered. Joseph could hear the grumbling from his workshop and, curious about what would agitate his neighbors that had nothing to do with him or Mary, he went to find out. As soon as he went out into the streets, he was approached.

"Caesar and Herod are not getting enough of our money?" asked one. "Now they want a census so they can make sure they tax every last one of us!"

"Rome demands I go to the place of my birth?" demanded another. "Who will do my work and mind my family while I spend two weeks traveling? Will they forgive my taxes for the time I am away, wasting my days?"

Joseph heard the man's wife, who had four children, murmur, "When will the Lord free us from all of this?

When will he send us the Messiah to end our captivity?"

But Joseph, when he finally learned the details of Caesar's decree, was secretly relieved. Though his business would suffer, there was nothing he wanted more right now than to get away from Nazareth. From the gossip about him and Mary. From the knowing looks and the bold stares. From the veiled and predatory glances of mothers with daughters old enough to be married. And, yes, from Mary herself. He didn't even mind the long journey to the place of his birth, David's city. He couldn't wait to leave for Bethlehem.

That night before going to sleep, he packed the provisions he would need and gave his mule an extra portion of feed. The poor creature had quite a journey ahead of him, but he was a loyal animal and would carry Joseph's provisions a lot easier than if Joseph had to bear them himself. Joseph would travel faster this way. He lay down to sleep, thinking that he might stay for a while in Jerusalem on the way back. By the time he returned to Nazareth, Mary's child might be born, and people would be anxious and interested by new things. He could find work in Jerusalem. For the first time in many weeks, he fell into a deep sleep.

But not a restful one, for well into the night, at its darkest hour, he wakened from a dream that left him at once breathless and excited and, most of all, terrified. Before dawn he was at the door of Joachim and Anna's home

66

where they and Mary still slept. It was Mary who roused herself first, hearing Joseph's voice calling in the dim morning, and came to the door. For the first time Joseph touched his wife, taking her arm and pulling her out into the chill morning, closer to him. Mary watched him, her eyes shining expectantly.

But now faced with her, he found himself unable to say all that he wanted to say. Still excited and anxious about the dream, he could not find the words to describe it, to tell her what the angel had said, and what he now *knew* to be true! He opened his mouth, but in his confusion and agitation could only stammer, "I have had a dream. I saw the angel! Mary, I believe you."

PRAY

St. Joseph, is there anyone in the life of Jesus who is a greater unsung hero than you? Is there a saint who has done more for Jesus, yet about whom we know less? You were the one who put your head down and kept working, kept doing the will of God, no matter how much you had to lose, no matter how demanding, no matter how completely the will of God went against the will of man—your will and the wills of those around you. We never hear of you questioning, resenting, lamenting, or even feeling sorry for yourself. When you left Nazareth, gloriously constrained with that holiest of burdens, the Son of God and his mother, you never once turned back, never once wondered when, or if, you would see your home and family again. Could I do what you did? Could I give so completely, so humbly, of myself? Could I be so kind, so generous, so uncomplaining? Help me, saint of all workers, to evince in my life the humility that you demonstrated in yours. Teach me to follow God relentlessly, no matter where he may lead me. Inculcate in me your humble nature that I may never put myself before others or before God's will. Help me to develop within myself just a fraction of your courage, compassion, strength, and perseverance. Amen.

ACT

Do something for Jesus that will provide you in return with no reward, no public approbation, no thanks, no glory, no honor. Try to focus your act on serving or helping a child in the same way that humble St. Joseph served Jesus. Donate anonymously to a school breakfast or lunch program. Bring groceries to a food pantry that serves families. The next time you are in a grocery store and see a parent behind you, quietly give the cashier extra money to help pay for his or her groceries, and leave before the transaction occurs. Do the same at a tollbooth: if you see a car behind you with children, pay their toll. Contribute to a charity that helps and heals children/families, especially those who live in the Middle East, which is still torn by the kind of violence and strife that characterized Joseph's time. Donate children's clothes and toys to a community program that serves low-income families. When you've made your act for Jesus in humility, thank him for the opportunity to serve and ask him to open your heart to continue to do his work, knowing that—like St. Joseph—your only reward will be knowing that you are doing God's will, which is the greatest reward of all.

QUESTIONS

1. Have you ever felt that God has spoken to you and asked you to do something that seemed impossible or even humiliating to you? What was your response?

2. How do we, as individuals or in community, respond to Jesus' radical call for Christian living as expressed in the gospels?

Five

BALTHASAR

In the time of King Herod, after Jesus was born in Bethlehem of Judea, wise men from the East came to Jerusalem, asking, "Where is the child who has been born King of the Jews? For we observed his star at its rising and have come to pay him homage."

MATTHEW 2:1–2

FOR WHAT SEEMED LIKE THE HUNDREDTH TIME SINCE HE'D LEFT HIS BEAUTIFUL, COMFORTABLE HOME, FILLED WITH THE TREASURES HE'D COLLECTED DURING A LIFE-TIME OF TRAVEL, BALTHASAR WONDERED WHY HE'D EVER TAKEN THE FIRST STEP OF THIS JOURNEY. Was it a fool's errand? Had they miscalculated? And what would be its end? On all the travels he'd undertaken in the past, with and without his current companions, he'd always known that he would gain something he desired by the end of the

trip. Riches. An alliance with a new king. Lucrative work. A
new instrument to better comprehend the story of nature
and the heavens. A priceless memento or artifact. And, best
of all, new knowledge.

But this journey? What would be its end?

He'd already spent a king's ransom on this enterprise, he
thought ironically, though he had no other objective for the
end of his journey—if indeed it had an end—than to offer
a gift of even greater value. Another expense! And this had
never been an inexpensive undertaking to begin with. He
was not an impetuous man; he did nothing without a great
deal of study and consideration. He and his companions
had spent three years on this venture, and though they had
collaborated in the past, never had they expended so much
time and wealth on a project whose end was so uncertain.

For over two years, they had studied the night skies, their
charts, the prophecies. They had talked and debated and
been silent, and then talked and debated and been silent
again, trying to understand what they were seeing, what the
natural world and the world of Scripture predicted. They
had tried to deny it, tried to disprove it, as was their way
when they tested a theory. They'd left no path unexplored in
examining their idea and their prospects for success. Then,
nearly a year ago, when there was nothing left to do but act or
surrender to the possibility of never knowing, they'd set out
to follow the light that had mesmerized all of them from the
moment of its relatively dim first appearance.

Not all of them set out, however. Most of the others
pleaded the expense, the uncertainty, their work, their

families, their reputations. But Balthasar and his two companions had not been able to resist, despite these challenges and difficulties. They had told each other that never in
their lives would they have another such opportunity. Their
studies and their experience assured them of this, if of little
else. They were among the wisest, most learned men in
the world; it would not be boasting, he knew, to declare
that truth. There were the others like them, the ones who'd
stayed behind, but all of them were men who had attained
and still sought great knowledge, the knowledge of things
that most people, in their fight just to survive, had not
time to seek or even imagine. Among the many people in
the wide world who knew of them, he and his companions
were simply called *the magi*.

But now the three of them who had plunged willingly into
this experiment—though it had advanced well beyond mere
experiment—grumbled at each other, wondering just how
wise they had been. The cost of their caravan had not given
them pause at first, but now, travel-weary and irritable, they
thought about it, talked about it, worried they'd made fools
of themselves. Each of the three had needed one camel for
provisions as well as two servants, the most loyal of their
men who would protect them and their riches even if it
meant dying for their masters. The journey would be long,
and the obvious wealth they carried would greatly tempt
every thief and vagabond they might meet along the way.
The world outside their own ornate palaces and holdings
was a dangerous one, and to none more so than men like
them who were brilliant in the ways of the mind and God's

heavens, but defenseless in the ways of most men. And then there was the price of the slave they'd brought to lead the other camel, laden with all that their three couldn't carry. Balthasar thought now also of the time and money they'd each spent selecting the gifts, those that were literally fit for a king. Still, each of the magi knew in the recesses of his heart that it was not the expense that truly distressed them now, many months into their traveling. After all, their reputations as the wisest in the world caused kings and rulers to pay well just to consult them. They lived lives of great luxury on the basis of their learning. No, it was not the money they'd spent; it was the fear that they might have been wrong, that this was nothing more than a foolish escapade, as Balthasar's first wife had told him.

"You are chasing your youth, my dear," she'd told him, waving a bejeweled hand languidly as he was making preparations to set out. She had been with him the longest, through his youth and early studies, and she knew him best of all his wives. "No matter how often you and the other two tell yourselves you are chasing the light in the night, the truth is you are fleeing age. Better to bring another wife into our household to serve us both and stay home where it is safe and comfortable."

Had she been right?

And yet.

If he and Melchior and Gaspar were right in their calculations, they would find something at the end of this journey beyond all riches.

The Messiah! The king of the Jews! The One that the

Israelites and the learned had been awaiting for millennia! If this passage truly ended at the palace of this king, they would have found the One whose coming had captivated the magi for generations, for as long as they'd known of him, just as he had commanded the hopes of the Jews for as long as they'd existed.

Few outside the people of Israel knew of the One to come, and many who did were pagans and did not believe. But the magi did believe. They had studied the history of the Jews, this now-oppressed and bedraggled nation who had started their existence in the delivering hand of the Great God. For centuries, for as long as the magi had found themselves in the world, they had been fascinated with the Israelites. Though no one considered it in these times—when for over a thousand years the Jews had been handed around from marauding nation to marauding nation like a worn wineskin at a wedding feast—they were once the proud people of the Great God. And the magi knew that the Great God had promised them, even now, that they would rise again, that he would send the One who would break their chains and free them from all the restraints of the world of men.

It was this One that they searched for, this One whose star had risen as the sign in the night sky that the prophecies were about to be fulfilled. Now they followed the star as it grew brighter, as the lights in the heaven came together, all in the service of the Great God. They'd been following it for months, through hot, airless days and freezing nights, through sand and wind storms, through long days of relentless, blinding sun. Balthasar had to admit, their spirits had failed them at times; was it just stubbornness that kept them going?

No. It was the chance to see the Great God's Messiah! The last time the Great God had reached out to free his people, it was through a mere man, Moses; and yet look what the Great God had accomplished through him! Plagues that devastated the powerful Egypt! Firstborn sons taken! The sea parted! And then, when the mere man, Moses, had finally brought the people to the land that the Great God had promised them, God went before them with a power and might that made every army cower and flee until God had cut a swath in the land wide and broad and deep enough for all his people, Israel.

If the Great God had done all that through the second son of a slave woman, Balthasar wondered in awe, what would he do through his very own Messiah?

"Where do you think we will find this One?" Melchior interrupted his reverie as they plodded along on their intrepid camels. It was a subject they discussed often and never seemed to tire of, probably because they had no an-swers. They could only speculate.

"He will be born in a city, there can be no question of that," said Gaspar, repeating an assertion he'd made from the beginning. "Where else can a king be born? Where else would there be riches enough to support him? His mother and father are surely highborn among the Jews and live well. Who can live well in the country or the desert?"

Gaspar's own palace was in the midst of his country's

largest city, of course, and he could conceive of no other possibility for the One they sought. Balthasar could not disagree; the three of them lived in the very centers of their own vibrant cultures, and they knew no learned or great family that lived far outside the centers of commerce and government.

"So it must be Jerusalem," said Melchior, "for the star is leading us in that direction, and it grows brighter by the day."

"It is what I have said from the first, before we even set out," Gaspar said complacently. "Where would the king of the Jews be born, if not Jerusalem?" Melchior sent his eyes heavenwards in a comical expression. Gaspar was often right, and he never let them forget even one instance.

"But would the One be born into captivity?" wondered Balthasar. "Why not Africa? What of the prophecy that says the Great God will call his Son out of Egypt?"

"Hah! Africa!" Gaspar exclaimed, and then, giving Balthasar a sidelong glance, added quickly, "Not that there is anything wrong with Africa, my good friend, but Egypt has seen its day. I think we can assume the Great God is done with Egypt."

"I don't think we can assume anything about the Great God," rejoined Melchior, "for many who have made assumptions about him in the past have suffered for their temerity."

This silenced Gaspar, though Balthasar could tell that he wanted to respond and held himself back with some difficulty. Balthasar had to suppress his own smile at Gaspar's discomfort. Melchior was the oldest among them, and even Gaspar had to concede that he was the wisest. They rode along silently for some time before Melchior spoke again. "I wonder if we will find him in a palace or just a magnificent dwelling filled with wealth?"

"A palace, of course," said Gaspar, always ready to re-assert himself. "Don't we three live in palaces? How can the Great God's Messiah be expected in any dwelling less favored than ours? We shall certainly not find him in a shepherd's hovel or a barn!" Gaspar chuckled, pleased with this image.

"Speaking of palaces, I am missing mine," sighed Melchior, shifting uncomfortably on his camel. Balthasar knew the trip had been hardest on his old friend, but Melchior seldom complained of physical ills. It was not the way of the magi to allow their bodies to constrain their seeking.

"But we are almost upon the place, I know it!" said Gaspar, determined to return to the point. "We must start to think about where to look when the star comes to a standstill. It has slowed in these past days. Should we not go now to Jerusalem?"

Melchior was silent for a moment and then said decisive-ly, "Let us send one of the men forward into Jerusalem to ask where the royal child has been born or, if he has not yet been born, where his mother resides. Surely, the Jews must be awaiting him as anxiously as we are."

Balthasar spoke slowly, "I am not sure we will find him in Jerusalem."

"You have never been sure!" Gaspar was frustrated. "You are never sure, always pondering, always wondering! Of course it must be Jerusalem. Look at the star!"

Though night had not yet fallen, the star was already visible, a white flame in the darkening indigo sky. It had indeed been moving in the direction of Jerusalem, but Balthasar knew that there was more than one city beneath that star. Still, if the Jews were preparing to meet their Messiah, there would at least be information to be found in Jerusalem. "By all means, my brothers," said Balthasar, "send the man ahead."

Two days later, their man had returned to them. They were a few hours journey away from the great captive city with its magnificent temple. Balthasar had always heard people talk of "going up to Jerusalem," and now he could see why. The city was built on a hill and shone like an earthly sun by night. Still, he could not help but notice that their star glowed brighter and was continuing to move, ever so slightly, over the city on the hill.

Their servant had surprising news. "Everyone I spoke to had heard of the prophecies about the Messiah, but no one seemed to know that this was the time! They were disturbed by my questioning, and a number of them sought me out. Many had noted the light in the sky, but none had your wisdom, Masters, to understand its meaning."

"Thank you for that recognition of our brilliance," Melchior said drily, handing the man the coin he expected.

Nonetheless, all three were stunned by this news, and not a little worried. How could the Jews not know about the advent of their Messiah? Or did this mean that the magi had indeed wasted years of their life?

"But perhaps," Melchior muttered, "we are not brilliant at all. And now, have we started an uproar in the captive city because of a mistake?"

"Wait, Masters!" cried the servant. "Just when I had given up hope of learning anything more, a messenger came from Herod, the ruler that the Romans have put in place. He calls himself a king, but the Jews seem to despise him almost as much as they do Caesar. They say that Caesar is the fist and Herod is Caesar's thumb upon them. But his messenger said that Herod had heard of my inquiries and was anxious to meet the great and renowned magi, of whom he has heard much. He wishes to do you honor, Masters, and asks that you dine with him tonight! Have I not done well?"

Clearly, thought Balthasar, by the man's shining, triumphant, upturned face, he thought he'd done very well, securing for his masters an invitation from the ruler of the region. But something dark and fearful stirred in Balthasar at the mention of Herod, and he could see the same distress reflected in the faces of his friends. Still, Melchior assured the servant they he had performed his duties well, and ordered the rest to prepare to go up to Jerusalem.

As the servants were busy getting the animals ready, the three magi moved a little distance away to confer. "You are not content, Melchior." For once Gaspar spoke with the respect the elder magi was due, and it was that more than anything that confirmed for Balthasar his own misgivings about this meeting.

"No," answered Melchior in a low voice. "I have heard of this Herod, this lackey of the Romans, and what I have heard does not comfort me. He is known as a vicious tetrarch, killing and enslaving his own people, though in reality they are not his. He taxes them grievously, adding to the burden from Rome, and he is known to turn a blind eye when Rome orders crucifixions to discourage rebellion."

This silenced them. Crucifixion was the most painful, shameful death a person could suffer, and it was only ordered for those in captive nations, never for Roman citizens. That a king, no matter how venal, would cooperate in such an execution of his own citizens was horrifying to them.

Gaspar tried to be encouraging. "But surely, Melchior, this Herod cannot be as wise as we, and especially not as wise as you. We are the magi, and have nothing to fear from..."

Melchior raised a hand to stop him. "My friends, Herod may not be as wise as us, but we are about to enter his world, and in his world, wisdom is nothing next to cruelty and barbarism. We must be on our guard; I sense there is more than we know about this invitation."

Balthasar agreed. "Can we not refuse Herod? Offer an excuse that we must continue our journey?"

"It would be an insult that he would not tolerate," Melchior answered. "He has heard of our quest, and we cannot afford to make an enemy of him. We are three men and a handful of servants in a foreign land. What could we do against a ruthless tyrant like Herod? No, we must go and match wits, magi against the king."

"Then I hope he feeds us well," said Gaspar grimly as he mounted his camel.

"I think you need not worry about that," answered Melchior. "I imagine King Herod sets an elaborate table."

"Indeed," said Balthasar, "but what will he require as payment for the feast?"

By nightfall they had left Herod, having courteously declined his offer to provide them with the most elegant of quarters in his elaborate palace. Herod had not wanted to let them go, but Melchior had carefully turned their refusal into a compliment that Herod could not deny by saying, "You have already given us enough of your time, good King Herod, and we know that your kindness to us keeps you from the significant duties a ruler as powerful as you must have. We would not be the cause of Caesar hearing that you dally with scholars when there is work to be done for Rome."

"What could he say to that?" Gaspar laughed gleefully as they rode slowly out into the night. "Was he to deny it and acknowledge that he has no other duties than to please Rome? It was quite clever of you, Melchior."

But the evening had been harrowing for them; Herod was determined to know where the child of the prophecies was to be born. Indeed, he wanted to know the time of the birth as well. For the first time since they'd begun to study the sacred texts and the star, the magi were grateful not to know where it would lead them. They could not tell Herod what they did not know, and they said as much to the king. Balthasar had seen the angry flame leap in Herod's eye when they'd denied all knowledge of where the child was or whether he had yet entered the world. It was only for an instant; in the next moment, Herod had masked his fury and resumed the mask of generous host and fellow seeker. But Balthasar, who by habit said little, had been watching the king closely from the moment they'd entered his presence, and he saw Herod's frustrated rage. He mentioned it now to his companions. Though they had not seen it, Melchior in particular felt a strong distrust for the king, though Herod had offered them a feast and entertainment unlike any they'd experienced since leaving their own countries.

"He says he wants to worship the newborn king of the Jews, but I have my doubts," Melchior mused. "I have never been questioned so avidly, even by another member of the magi. And I think he lies when he says that he, too, has long sought this Messiah. There is something evil in Herod, something that makes my very skin crawl as though covered with fire ants. He does not wish this newborn child well. I was glad we could tell him no more than when the star appeared."

"I do not think he will stop his search with us," said Balthasar. "Our quest has awakened something in him. He is on fire to find the child, and though he claims it is with sincere longing, I don't believe him either."

"Oh, Herod is longing for something, certainly, but it is not the welfare of the child," said Melchior somberly. "Did you see the fear in him? He hid it well, but not from me. Were it not for that fear, he would never have let us leave his palace alive."

"What have we started?" asked Balthasar. "Have we endangered the very One we came to seek and worship?"

Gaspar, filled with Herod's fine food and spiced wine, was not convinced of the king's malice. "Surely, the temporal ruler of the captive Jews would welcome the birth of the One who will free Israel. Would he not be seeking the kingdom of God?"

"Herod seeks for Herod and nothing else," said Balthasar. "This man is far from the Great God. I think the last thing he wants is to meet the Great God's Chosen One."

"Then, it is a good thing that we don't know where he will be born?" Gaspar still sounded doubtful.

"For now, it is a good thing." Melchior was certain.

"And we will not return to Herod, as he asked, when we find the child?" Gaspar persisted.

"We will not," Melchior declared forcefully, and Balthasar hid a smile at Gaspar's crestfallen expression. His companion did love a well-laden table.

They all three looked up at the shimmering light that lately had eclipsed all other lights in the heavens. Though it had hardly moved now for days, it was still, almost imperceptibly, slipping south of Jerusalem. At least once every night, as at this moment, they—among the few who knew what it meant—were overcome by awe at the sight.

"Where is it going? Where is he who will be born the king of the Jews?" Gaspar whispered reverently.

"Not in Jerusalem." Balthasar urged his camel out through the city gates.

PRAY

Lord Jesus, you both fulfilled every messianic prophecy and defied every messianic expectation! You were the long-awaited guest and the unexpected party crasher. You came to rich and poor, well and ill, powerful and powerless. You were what the world most waited for and what the world least anticipated. As Simeon told Mary when she presented you at the temple, and as Herod and other worldly rulers would soon discover, you came for the rising and the falling of many in power. Lord, help me to defy the limitations of my own human nature and seek to follow you, just as you defied the limitations of what a king should be. Help me to be forgiving when my human nature calls out for vengeance, help me to be kind when my sinful nature wants to be mean, help me to be generous when my human fear seeks to be stingy, and help me to find your peace when the things of this world make me anxious. Amen.

ACT

What gift will you bring Jesus for his birthday this year? Take some time away from your Christmas shopping list for others to consider what to give the Lord of the Feast. The magi brought the magnificent royal treasures of frankincense, myrrh, and gold, but were those the most important gifts they gave the Christ Child? Was it not rather the gift of their time: the time they spent studying Scripture, the time they took away from their daily lives and work and families to seek him, the time they devoted to finding and worshiping him despite the ignorance and protests of the rest of the world? Give Jesus the gift of your time this Christmas. Spend precious minutes with him at the beginning or the end of every day. Visit him in the Blessed Sacrament. Spend time praying or just observing at a Christmas manger scene. Give him what, for many of us, is the hardest gift to spare: your time. And remember that every second of it is from him, so we are only giving back a fraction of what is already his.

QUESTIONS

1. Have you ever taken a great risk to pursue something deeply important to you, even when others didn't understand or agree? What was it? How did it work out?

2. What risks are we willing to take to seek, find, and follow Jesus in our time, in "real" time?

Six

HEROD

*When King Herod heard this, he was frightened, and
all Jerusalem with him; and calling together all the
chief priests and scribes of the people, he inquired of
them where the Messiah was to be born. They told him,
"In Bethlehem of Judea, for so it has been written by the
prophet."* MATTHEW 2:3–5

HEROD'S SLAVES SCATTERED, ALL SEEKING THEIR OWN
HIDING PLACES, THE CORNERS AND TRUNKS AND CREV-
ICES IN WHICH THEY HAD OFTEN FOUND SAFETY DURING
THEIR MASTER'S TANTRUMS. Still, they had never seen
him quite as insanely furious as he was now that the magi
had gone. The rage had been burning in him for days, since
he'd heard of the wise men's search, and it had simmered in
him during the banquet he'd given for them, probing them
to no avail. But it had only risen to a fever pitch this night

when he'd realized that the magi would not be returning
as he'd instructed them. They had escaped his reach. They
would not be telling him what he wished to know.

Where was the child of the prophecy?

He had wanted to scream it in their faces, to roast them
as his cooks had roasted the lamb the magi willingly de-
voured, until they told him the place—not just the city, but
the very dwelling! Now, as he sensed their intent to escape
him, he wanted to recapture them, torture them, scourge
them, to make them pay for bringing this quest to his very
doorstep and then not providing the answer to the dangerous question of where. Where was the One?

But Herod was too wily to pursue any such course with
the magi. He knew them by reputation, and he did not dare
bring the world down upon himself by mistreating even
one of these brilliant and highly regarded men. They were
almost a legend; he himself had never met one of the magi
before, but he well knew that there were only a handful of
these powerful men in the world, and he couldn't risk being
the one who harmed any of their society. Rome would not
look kindly on a ruler who brought such censure and chaos
to its captive lands.

And Herod, at heart a superstitious coward, wasn't sure
he could destroy the magi. With all his power, all his soldiers, all his innate cruelty and wit, he was still not certain
that such men could be interfered with, and he did not
dare find out. So he'd curbed his temper in their presence,
though even then he'd had the disconcerting sense that
they knew what he was just below the smooth surface he

presented them, and that they distrusted him for the raging envy they discerned in him. No matter how he'd plied them with delicacies, spices, wine, and flattery, they had grown more inscrutable with every passing minute of the feast, until his own blood had boiled within him, so that even he, glutton that he was, did not enjoy the food.

Finally, in a desperate effort to reassure his near-silent guests, he'd said in as sweet a voice as he could manage with blood pounding through his veins and beating in his ears, "My friends, I am no more than you in this: I seek the Holy One of Israel so that I, too, might worship him. *When you have found him, bring me word, so that I can go and pay him homage*" [Matthew 2:8]. At these false words, the one from Africa, called Balthasar, raised his eyes for a single moment to Herod's face, and in that moment, Herod saw the loathing and comprehension he feared.

By the time they'd gone, still not providing him with even the smallest hint, he was beside himself. But such distress was nothing compared to what he felt when his spies had told him a few hours later that the magi might well have eluded him. They were gone by night, as they'd come. His cringing spies had hardly scurried from the room before he erupted, overturning tables and scattering the remains of the evening meal throughout the dining chamber. He hurled the golden plates against the tapestries, shattered the goblets, and tore the draperies. His slaves, cowering as far away as they dared go, heard his mania and, already resigned to the cleaning they would have to do when he'd spent his fury, prayed only for their own safety.

Many a slave of Herod's had been maimed or even executed when the tetrarch was in the throes of his temper.

When he'd done as much damage as he could manage and had screamed himself nearly hoarse, he sent for Simon, the head of the royal household. The beleaguered man came reluctantly, having felt the considerable sting of his master's anger in the past, but knowing he had no choice. Herod provided well for him and his family, and Simon already had two small sons, with another child on the way. Besides, Simon well knew that none in Herod's household could refuse such a summons and live. His wife would not thank him for defying Herod and losing his head along with her means of support. He bowed his way into the shattered and food-stained chamber, where Herod now sat in the midst of the ruin, calm and intensely focused. The king seemed to be deliberately ignoring the devastation he'd caused all around him, but Simon knew better. His master was perfectly unaware of his surroundings; now that he'd done the damage, it meant nothing to him. It didn't exist.

Simon knew better than to reveal that he noticed anything amiss in the chamber or, for that matter, in the king. He stood silently before Herod, his eyes fixed on the floor, and awaited the king's wishes. They were not long in coming. Herod did not deign to look upon Simon as he issued his directive. "Fetch into my presence my scholars, my priests, my rabbis, my learned men. Fetch all those under my rule who are versed in Scripture. Fetch those who know the ways of the magi. I want them immediately."

Simon knew better than to argue that it was late at night,

that all such men would not be easy to find or reach at such an hour. He did not ask whether they could be brought in the morning, or whether he might be given more time to find those who might be reticent or reclusive. He did not ask how Herod intended to reward these men or even whether the king would provide them with lodging or food. He did not dare. Simon merely assented and bowed his way out of the room. He only drew a full breath when he was out of Herod's presence and as he girded himself for the coming hours and days. He knew he would not sleep for a long time. But he could not know how long it would be before he ever truly rested again.

Herod, however, slept well and peacefully, much as an infant who wears himself and his parents out with shrieking will sleep after tormenting the household and all the neighbors. Thus the king appeared rested and powerful when all the learned men of his province came into his presence, having heard about his frustrated attempt to draw information from the magi. The room had been transformed by the slaves who'd crept out of their hiding holes to feverishly clear and clean away all signs of their master's distemper. Everything was gleaming, and the torn and stained tapestries had been replaced. Herod was dressed in his finest raiment, a jewel-crusted crown on his oiled head, a scepter in his hand. As if, thought Simon, anyone could forget who was the king in the room.

Some of the learned men now summoned to this room showed their fear openly, knowing that Herod would be pleased to see them tremble in his sight; others strove to present a confident visage to the tetrarch, hoping to win his favor by a demonstration of arrogance. At these Simon repressed a sour smile, for no one knew better than he that they hoped in vain. But Herod looked over them all with a cold, calculating eye, and Simon, standing apart beside the newly hung tapestries, knew that this roomful of clever men had no idea what their king was capable of. They had heard rumors, yes, but they had not seen as he, Simon, had seen. This was a ruthless tyrant who had slaughtered members of his own family to retain control and ensure obedience. These scholars were nothing to him, and woe to them if they could not do his bidding.

Herod did not bother to address them, having already given his instructions to Simon. Now, nodding once at Simon, Herod merely surveyed the gathering as the head of his household spoke his words. Not one of them turned to look at Simon; they kept their eyes fixed on Herod as Simon's announcement rang through the chamber.

"Your king has honored you by calling you into his presence to test your knowledge. He has dined with the wisest men in the world, the magi, and he wishes to know if his learned men are of the same quality as these. He poses to you the same question he posed to the magi: where is the Messiah of God to be born?"

The scribes and scholars could not help themselves. Instantly murmurs and discussions broke out among them.

Simon heard scattered words and phrases, some louder than others: "only in the city of David"..."He shall be called a Nazarene"..."Nazareth! Never!"..."the Light is to come from Galilee"..."Elijah must return first"..."yes, yes, Isaiah, but we cannot ignore Jeremiah"..."and what about Egypt?"

Herod silenced them instantly by abruptly rising. Menace seemed to pour off his figure like a wind-driven fog. "I am not interested in your endless haggling, your relentless debates. I want one answer, not a dozen," he snarled. "And I want it within the hour." Then he swept from the room, leaving the men speechless. Simon was grimly amused to see the changing looks on the faces of those who had been most arrogant. Now they turned to him, terrified, their faces upturned in supplication. Do they really think I can help them? he wondered; do they really know so little about their king? One of the eldest rabbis pleaded as though Simon could intercede for them: "Even if we can come to agreement on the likely place, no one can be certain!"

He turned away from their fear, saying gruffly, "You had better be."

Two hours later, at the break of dawn, Simon had called a new group of Herod's men to the king's chamber. Herod's soldiers were a rough lot, powerfully built and cruel-natured men, for who else could do the bidding of a tetrarch like Herod? Their leaders now slouched about the king's quarters, waiting for Herod, ac-

customed to being summoned at his whim. Simon knew
the officer in charge of the guard; they were of the same
age, and the man had a very young son who played with
Simon's children. Simon had come to think of this officer as
decent despite his dedication to Herod. He did not lounge
about like his colleagues, but stood at attention although
Herod had not yet appeared. Impatient, he now turned to
Simon. "What is this about? Has it to do with the magi?" he
asked in a low voice, for all of Jerusalem knew by now of the
wise men's search for the prophesied king of the Jews and
their visit with Herod.

Though Simon would have liked to tell him, he didn't
really know. Herod had received an answer from the terrified scholars in private and, having dismissed them, had
summoned Simon and directed him to call the leaders of
his guard. Simon had roused the men out of their beds, en-
during the abuse of all but their officer, and brought them
to the antechamber to await the king. He told the man as
much, but he could see that the officer was troubled. "If it is
about the magi, my men won't be easily persuaded to pursue them," he told Simon urgently. "Nothing short of death
will force them to hunt these foreigners whom they believe
have skills beyond those of mere men. If Herod..." But
before he'd finished speaking, Herod arrived, announced by
his attendants. Immediately, the leaders of the guard stood
at attention, their faces carven masks of unthinking duty.

Herod did not even glance at Simon, nor did he give him
the words he wished spoken to the guard. The king merely
gestured for Simon and the officer to follow him into the in-

ner chamber. There, out of the hearing of the others, Herod spoke directly to his commander, still ignoring Simon, who began to feel a deep dread grow within him. It was not that he disliked being out of Herod's mind; he positively relished those moments when the king ignored him and left him in peace. But there was something in Herod's manner that made his flesh creep. Never before had Herod conceived a plan so evil that he felt it necessary to exclude Simon in its execution. There was a darkness in Herod's eyes, an uncharacteristic stillness in his demeanor that at first stymied Simon.

Until he recognized it as madness.

"I have asked the magi to return to me when they find the child they search for, but I think it unlikely that they will come back. Thus am I repaid by these foreigners for my hospitality." Herod smiled coldly, his voice low and even. "I will give them a few more days to remember the meaning of courtesy and return with the answer I seek, but I hold out little hope."

Herod paused for so long that it was difficult for Simon and the officer to refrain from exchanging glances. After some time the king, now shifting his unseeing gaze to a place beyond the two men before him, asked the officer, "Have you any particularly brutal men?" His tone was so light that he might have been asking if the man wanted wine. In a swift sidelong glance, Simon saw the officer conceal his shock, and in the next moment, he answered, "All of your soldiers live to serve you, my king."

Herod's eyes fixed upon him as swiftly as a hawk dives

upon a dove. "And you, commander? Do you live to serve your king?" The voice retained its light, playful tone, but there was something deadly here, and Simon felt it in his very soul.

The officer replied in a voice devoid of all emotion. "The king knows I live to serve him."

Herod smiled thinly. "That is as it should be. But then, why avoid my question? I have had quite enough of men avoiding my questions. How many soldiers do you have who will stop at no act, no matter how barbaric, to serve me? And don't tell me all, because I know what I ask, and the answer is not all."

Simon heard the officer draw a long breath, taking a moment to recover himself. "There are some men, not many, my king, in every guard, for whom violence and depravity is part of their nature. They are fit for nothing else."

"And make the most loyal soldiers, I should think," said Herod pointedly. When neither the head of his household nor the commander of his guard responded, he narrowed his eyes. Murderous rage darkened his features, and Simon feared that they would die in this chamber. But when Herod instantly recovered and next spoke with chilling calm, Simon wanted to die.

"If the magi do not have a change of heart and do their duty to me, I must take this matter into my own hands. Rome will not tolerate the confusion and unrest caused by rumors of another king. It is my unfortunate role to protect my people, to be a father to them. Sometimes a father must act decisively, to make sacrifices to protect the family. My family is large. Small sacrifices must be made. Commander, find the men who will kill all boys under the age of two in Bethlehem. Do not yet tell them what they must do, but keep them at the ready. Be sure they have plenty of meat and wine. Await my decree."

Herod left the chamber without another word. He had not once glanced at Simon. The two men, young fathers each, stood paralyzed. It seemed an eternity before each could raise his eyes to the other's bloodless face. Even then neither could speak. Finally, Simon, as if in a trance, said in a raw voice, "The scribes and rabbis he called in last night overlooked a prophecy when they gave him their answer."

The officer, still numb with shock, gave him a questioning look. Simon whispered in horror: "*Thus says the Lord: A voice is heard in Ramah, lamentation and bitter weeping. Rachel is weeping for her children; she refuses to be comforted for her children, because they are no more*" [Jeremiah 31:15].

PRAY

Merciful Father, the rage and fear and jealousy of Herod is hard to behold and even more horrifying to think about. Lord, how much agony has been caused in the world by the combination of fear and envy with power! Forgive us, Lord,

*for the devastation we cause through our pitiful human
nature; forgive us as nations, forgive us as cities, forgive
us as churches, forgive us as religions, forgive us as communities, forgive us as individuals. Lord, forgive me for the
many times my fear of losing control of my life or my mate-
rial goods has prompted me to jealousy or anger, and have
mercy on me, Father, for the times I've allowed those feelings
to corrupt my actions and my relations with others. Help me
to understand—and live—the simple truth that in seeking
you, I have my life's work and all that matters. Envy has no
place or purpose in this lifelong quest. Amen.*

ACT

As you shop for Christmas presents, add someone to
your list whom you are or have been jealous of. If you had
not planned to give this person a gift, all the better. Do
not give a present that may be perceived as grudging or a
thinly veiled insult; in other words, forget the costly pot of
anti-aging cream, no matter how expensive the lotion or
prestigious the brand! As you consider what to give, think
carefully about the person. Look beyond those things or
aspects of his or her personality that motivated your envy.
Does he love to read? Buy a title you know he would like, or
a gift certificate to a bookstore he frequents. Does she love
theater? Buy her tickets to a new play (and maybe offer to
accompany her if you think you can manage to enjoy the
evening). Make it clear—to God, your giftee, and yourself—
from your gift that you've put your mind and heart into it.

QUESTIONS

1. Have you ever felt compelled by a worldly authority to do something that you believed was against Jesus and his teachings? How did you deal with it?

2. What should be the Christian community's response to government policies that contradict Jesus' teachings?

Seven

The SERVING GIRL

While they were there, the time came for her to deliver
her child. And she gave birth to her firstborn son and
wrapped him in bands of cloth and laid him in a
manger, because there was no place for them in the inn.

LUKE 2:6–7

HER MASTER LAUGHED LOUDLY, FALSELY, AS THOSE
POOR, HUNGRY TRAVELERS WHO HAD PAID HIS NEWLY
RAISED PRICES WERE NOW COMPLAINING ABOUT THE
HIGH COSTS AND POOR SERVICE AT HIS CROWDED INN.
"What are you upset about, my brothers and sisters?" he
asked with deceitful friendliness. "Have I not provided you
with excellent accommodations given the circumstances?
Is it my fault that Caesar ordered a census? Am I the one
who forced you to return to your ancestor David's poor,

little city of Bethlehem? Have I not my own living to make, or am I to suffer because you need a place to stay while you are counted by the Roman oppressors? Am I to offer lodgings for free? And have I not prepared for you the finest, the most tender, of lamb and lentil pottages from the most perfect ewes of the flock? Do I not serve you the thickest, tastiest curds from the freshest goat's milk?"

His words were met with groans and derision, some good-natured, some not, from the men and families he had packed into his inn like grapes in a press. The serving girl heard one of them shout, "Tender lamb and lentil pottage? From the most perfect ewes? I've tasted more tender meat from rams that died of old age!" The laughter at this was raucous, and an older woman, encouraged by the crowd, called out, "As have I! And I almost broke a tooth on the stones in these perfect lentils of yours, innkeeper!"

The serving girl smiled to herself, secretly pleased that these poor souls saw through the mask of her greedy master. He'd been overjoyed when Caesar had issued his decree, and knowing full well that those needing to return to Bethlehem would be desperate for lodging, he had doubled his prices. "What choice will they have but to pay whatever I ask?" he'd said gleefully when word of Rome's decree reached Bethlehem. But now her master, annoyed at the scorn of his lodgers and seeing the smile flit across her weather-roughened features, yanked her aside where no one could see his exaggerated smile twist into a sneer.

"Will you think it so amusing if I cast you out and give your job to another, more respectful girl?" he snarled. "Or perhaps you'd prefer to be with your wretched, rag-clad brothers minding the sheep on this cold night?"

The truth was she'd much rather be free and in the open country with her brothers and the other shepherds, but she'd been told time and again that minding the flock was men's work and no place for a woman. Her father had made that abundantly clear, and her mother, worn out with childbearing and household work, had offered nothing to gainsay him. The serving girl especially longed to see the light in the dark sky that her youngest brother had spoken of recently, a light that he said had moved slowly toward them over the many past nights. She never tired of listening to his awestruck description, and she liked to imagine this wonder. She'd even thought she'd glimpsed this strange star herself as she came to the inn earlier, but when she'd excitedly mentioned it, her master had dismissed it as the imaginings of her dim mind.

"Any fool can see a star in the sky; any fool can see thousands," he'd said dismissively. "Instead of watching the sky, keep your eyes and mind on your work."

Still, as long as this crowd remained in Bethlehem for the census, she knew she had nothing to fear from her master. Who else could he hire who would be willing to work like a dog as she did? He must have seen this confidence in her silent, sullen expression, for he squinted suspiciously at her and gave her arm a twist. "Bring a pitcher of goat's milk to that group in the corner," he ordered, adding in a quiet hiss, "and make sure you water it down. They can complain all they want, but where else can they go for a meal and lodging this late?" This, at least, brought a genuine smile to his face, but she turned away from it, disgusted. As he hurried off to greet yet another weary family with their purse already opened, she took the opportunity to ladle a full serving of unadulterated milk into the pitcher for the hungry children in the corner.

When she looked up she saw the new couple.

No older than herself, the girl leaned heavily on the older man, probably the husband, her face contorted in pain. Noting the billowing robes the husband gathered protectively around his wife, the serving girl knew immediately the cause of her agony. She was heavy with child, and likely in the first throes of the birth pangs. She hurried over to them, but had hardly heard the husband's desperate plea, "A room? Anywhere?" before her master, noting in one practiced glance their poverty, strode over and dismissed them with an abrupt wave.

"There is no room in my inn. Look elsewhere."

The husband, his face creased with worry, was turning away, anxious to find shelter somewhere, when the child-wife opened her eyes from a wrenching grimace and met the serving girl's startled gaze. Neither spoke, but in that moment the serving girl felt that all she had ever been and ever would be and ever could be was known by this pain-wracked girl in whose eyes was a light to rival any star her brother had seen.

The serving girl gripped her master's arm. He tried to shake her off, but she would not have it.

"Give them the stable."

He laughed unpleasantly. "I just said there is no room here, or have you gone deaf as well as dumb? Mind your work. This has nothing to do with you."

"Give them the stable or you can serve this mob yourself."

He stared at her, first outrage and then a hint of fear flickering over his features as he saw a girl who was no longer his servant staring back at him. Glancing furtively at the raucous, demanding crowd of lodgers, he licked his lips nervously. Turning his back to her, he spoke roughly to the husband, "There is a stable out back. Take it if you must."

The young wife smiled weakly, gratefully, at her, and the serving girl, hardly aware of what she was doing, nodded back at her. As her master started to walk away, she said quickly, "I will show them."

He whirled back upon her. "You are here to work," he growled. "They can find it themselves."

She held his gaze, her head high. "I will show them." She paused, again thrilled to see the confusion in his face. "It won't take long. I'll be right back."

Taking advantage of his silence and not waiting for a response, she took the wife by the arm and started to lead her to the back entrance. The husband followed silently, though she thought she could feel the gratitude in his gaze. She was relieved to hear one of the more unhappy lodgers start an argument with her master; that would keep him busy for a while.

"My name is Mary," the girl said softly, "and my husband is Joseph. Thank you."

"Don't thank me," the serving girl said wryly. "You haven't seen what that thief calls a stable. It's barely more than a cave."

"It's better than anything we might have found elsewhere at this point," the man said, as he helped his young wife clamber over the debris strewn in the back of the inn. "There is not much time."

The stable was just a few minutes walk away, but it took longer because Mary was unable to move quickly. After she bit back a small cry of pain, the man lifted her into his arms and followed the serving girl into the entrance of an unkempt grotto. It was a place where the inn's animals sheltered, and there was fresh straw and grain for their food. Although the night was cold, the rude structure provided sturdy shelter away from the wind. The space was warmed a little by the animals, and the serving girl, who had brought a candle, lit several lanterns that cast a fairly strong glow.

Seeing the animals, Joseph's eyes widened and the serving girl felt ashamed that this was the best she had been able to do for them. "I'm sorry," she stammered, seeing his distress. But he cut her off. "No, no, it's not the place. I just remembered I left our animal out front. I was so worried, I forgot. Can you...can you spare a few more minutes and stay with her until I fetch it and return?"

"Joseph, don't worry," the young wife smiled through her pain, "I'll be fine. We can't keep her any longer. She has risked enough to help us."

Immediately he nodded. "Mary's right. Forgive me. You

must get back or you'll lose your work."

The serving girl laughed ruefully. "Go. Get your animal and bring it back here. I'll wait with her. After what I said to him, he will not keep me beyond the need caused by Caesar's census. Once this rush of lodgers is gone, he will get rid of me, too."

Joseph looked pained at this, but the serving girl gestured him away. When he'd gone, she helped Mary settle into the warmest corner. "Mary," she asked, suddenly shy and unsure how to say what she was thinking. "You are young, and I think this is your first?"

The young wife nodded, and the serving girl felt emboldened. "Have you…have you seen birth before?"

"Yes," Mary gasped at the crest of a pain, "my cousin. She was very old to bear a child, but he was her first and the birth went well."

The serving girl looked at her. "And you are very young. This may not be as easy. Do you want me to try to get help?" The serving girl was thinking of her own mother, though she knew her mother would not welcome being called out into the night for a stranger. Just yesterday she was grumbling about all the "strangers" in Bethlehem for the census.

Mary said, "I have Joseph."

"Yes, but he is a man. A good man, I can see that, but still, a man. I can try to find a woman from the village. Or…"

Mary smiled gently. "The child will be fine. I will be fine. Believe me. I know this to be true. I think it will be a few hours before he comes."

"I'll be finished at the inn by then," said the serving girl,

thinking to herself, *if not before then, and probably for good!*
"I'll come to you afterward. I'll bring some blankets. Also
curds and milk. You'll need to eat for strength."

Mary nodded. "I'll look for you." And the serving girl was
surprised at how pleased she felt at the young wife's words.
Joseph came in then, having tethered their animal at the
cave's entrance. Before returning to the inn, she showed
him where to find the water pump in the yard and where it
was safe to build a small fire.

"Thank you." Joseph looked very grave, and the servant
girl, feeling sorry for him, asked, "Are you afraid?"

"I am. Not about the birth, but about…what comes after."

She looked at him in surprise. "But tonight will be the
hardest thing."

Joseph smiled sadly at her, and suddenly she could see
every difficult mile they had traveled in the lines of his face.
"Tonight? No. Tonight is only the beginning." And before
she could question him again, he'd turned away toward the
grotto.

She began to hurry toward the inn, which seemed to
throw a garish light into the darkness. She could hear the
voices and arguments within. Her steps slowed. Suddenly,
it was the last place she wanted to be. She wished she could
go now to the hills and find her younger brother. She would
have her own story to tell this night, in the clear chill air
under the stars.

The stars! She looked up, and saw what she'd only
glimpsed earlier in the night. It was the light—the star!—
that her brother had been talking about these past months.

Her lips parted and a soft cry escaped at the sight, for it was like nothing she'd ever seen before. *This* was what they were all talking about! How often had she returned home at night after her drudgery and not bothered to lift her tired eyes from the rough ground in front of her? And all the while she'd been missing *this*! But then she remembered her brother's words as if he were standing beside her.

"It was small at first, and so far away. It seemed like just another light in the dark sky. There are thousands, millions, I cannot count them. I don't have enough numbers in my mind. But this one moved differently than the others. With the other lights, it is the same season after season, year after year. You needn't be a magi or one of Herod's scholars to know this; every shepherd knows the night sky. But this star was different. Over the months it became brighter, *and it moved closer*! To Bethlehem? To me! If I wanted to be named a fool, I might have thought it was coming to me, answering my call. At first our brothers took no notice, except to chide me for my foolishness. But in these past weeks even they—even the eldest among us, *especially* the eldest—study it. It glows and glimmers and seems to shoot light from its very core. What is it? What does it mean? We can hardly keep our eyes on the flock for watching it."

The serving girl understood now. Finally, she knew what he meant. She was seeing it for herself. Tentatively at first, and then eagerly, she lifted her hand toward the star. It was so bright, so low in the sky, she thought she might touch it! It seemed to lower itself toward her! Her hand trembled.

"You! Girl! I am out of patience! Get in here now and

help with these wretches! Or you will see no wages. Am I to do everything on my own?" Her master was silhouetted in the back doorway of the inn, an angry, ridiculous figure.

Her hand fell. The star seemed to recede back into the sky. But not far. It shone over her, and she prayed that some of its light would find a way into the grotto where Mary lay. Perhaps she would take comfort in it.

The serving girl turned back to the inn. Her master stayed long enough to see that she obeyed and then disappeared inside only to be greeted by shouts and more grumbling. The serving girl smiled. It didn't matter anymore to her. She no longer yearned to be in the fields with her brothers, but only to talk with them of the star and its meaning. As she entered the hot, crowded inn, she was already thinking of what she would bring later, in a few hours, to help Mary and Joseph. There were some old linens, well used, but clean and soft; she had washed them herself. Then, there was the supper her master grudgingly allowed her after her work was finished—never before! She would set it aside. That would do well for Mary and Joseph, who probably had eaten very little today.

She thought of the lovely, soft shawl her mother had made for her, a gift at last year's Passover. She had been surprised; her mother was not one to give presents. Nor did she have the time to make something so delicate or the inclination to spend money on the softest wool. Her mother must have noticed her astonishment, because her creased face colored and she gave her daughter a small smile. "Your grandmother made one like this for me on Passover when I was nearly your age," she'd said almost shyly. "For your own journey someday. May you go with the Lord."

For some reason, the serving girl had taken the shawl with her tonight, though she seldom wore it to work. She had placed it carefully in a high, seldom-used cupboard where it would not be stained or stolen. She thought of the child to be born and how it would feel against the infant's skin.

She plunged into the boisterous crowd inside, happy to be among them, warmed by the knowledge that in a few hours she would be out under the star again on her way to Mary and Joseph. She would help them.

How could she, who'd slaved for others all her life, know that for the first time she would discover what it really meant to serve?

PRAY

Lord Jesus, you were born to free all people from the restraints of the world in order to make us better able to follow you. You have asked us, Lord, to put service to you and each other before everything else in our lives. Lord, I am like the serving girl: my world seems so busy and full of distractions, small and large, especially at this time of year as I prepare to celebrate your birthday. Help me to remember, in the midst of all that is happening, that you are to be the center of my life. From you flows all that I need. Free me, Lord, from anything that holds me back from true service to you. Amen.

ACT

Is some issue or problem—a difficult job, a broken relationship, a lingering sin—holding you back from celebrating and embracing the freedom inherent in Jesus' birthday? Take time in these precious days and starlit nights before Christmas to release what is troubling you about this situation, knowing that Jesus came to free you from it. Imagine yourself laying this obstacle—whatever it is and whatever is causing it—at the foot of the manger. Now walk away, leaving it there as you follow Jesus on the journey that will soon begin.

QUESTIONS

1. When have you struggled with a work situation, including work you do at home as a spouse or parent? How does—or how did—your relationship with Jesus inform that struggle?

2. When you reach out beyond your comfort level to help another or others, do you consider that you are doing God's work? How does that make you feel?

Eight

The SHEPHERD BOY

In that region there were shepherds living in the fields,
keeping watch over their flock by night. Then an angel
of the Lord stood before them, and the glory of the Lord
shone around them, and they were terrified. LUKE 2:8–9

HE ONLY WISHED HIS SISTER COULD SEE THE STAR AS IT
WAS NOW, GLOWING JUST ABOVE THEM, SHIMMERING
AND SPARKING, SENDING OFF RAYS OF BRIGHT LIGHT,
EVEN WARMING THE NIGHT SO THAT A MIST ROSE UP
FROM THE LAND AROUND THEM. For so long she had
been the only one willing to listen to him speak of it. For
months his brothers and the other shepherds had laughed
at him, called his fascination a thing only a child would feel.
It was true: he was the youngest. Always the youngest. The

youngest brother, the youngest among those tending flock, the youngest even among those boys who were allowed to go the festivals in Jerusalem. He was so tired of being the youngest. Didn't he work as hard as the others? Didn't he do his share? Did he ever shirk his duty to the flock, even when it meant chasing away the wild animals that would scatter or kill them? But what credit did he get for all this? None. The only one who didn't treat him like a child was his sister.

She'd shared his secret pleasure when the star had proved him right. He didn't dare show his brothers a triumphant face; they would have never tolerated such a display of arrogance from him. Nevertheless, he could not help but rejoice within himself—and, quietly, with his sister—several weeks past when the other shepherds started taking notice of the peculiar light in the sky. His brothers continued to pretend it was nothing just to spite him, but even they had to show respect when the older shepherds began to remark upon the star and its unheralded course in the heavens. Shepherds, particularly the oldest, were not given to much speech. When they spoke, it was about the flock or the weather, anything that might affect the sheep. Perhaps if one had brought something good to eat, there would be a comment, but not much beyond that. Shepherds didn't put their trust in words. They said as much to their dogs as they did to each other. That had been the hardest thing for him about being a shepherd: not the cold nights or the hard work or the danger from thieves and wolves, but the silence. How he wished he could work with his sister in the crowded, noisy inn where people did nothing but talk and debate and joke! How he wished he could be the center of such constant activity and excitement. Of course, he didn't dare say that aloud. His brothers, not to mention his mother and father, would show no mercy on a boy who wanted to trade places with his sister! So, he quelled this desire and, in the fields and hills, he had learned to bite back more than he said. Still, he talked more than any of the others. This was another mark of his childishness, his brothers teased him, though most of the others tended to simply smile indulgently at his chatter.

So when the older ones started taking notice of the star—remarking on it!—the shepherd boy felt vindicated. Even his brothers were forced to acknowledge its presence. Then, tonight, the unthinkable happened! Just before sunset as the twilight was falling, he and his brothers were stunned to see their father coming toward them through the wilderness! Instantly the boy's heart had started pounding in his chest. What had happened? Never before had his father come to them in the hills. His parents hardly had time to speak with them on the rare occasions when they were able to leave the flock for a visit home or to attend a festival. His father, he'd thought often, might as well have been a shepherd, for all the talking he did.

So the sight of him hurrying toward them had shocked and worried all three brothers. But the youngest thought first of his sister. Something terrible had befallen her! She was sick, or perhaps even dead! His breath caught in his throat, and a hidden part of him was forced to admit that he'd rather lose any member of his family before his sister.

She was only a year older than he, but he loved her more than anyone, even his parents. She was the only one he could be himself with. Lately he had been worried because his mother was constantly telling her she must marry soon and leave their house. They needed the room and wanted one less mouth to feed. He wondered if her husband would welcome a younger brother when he wanted to visit. Somehow, he doubted this.

He and his brothers went to meet their father, the other shepherds following at a distance, not wanting to interfere but also curious about what would bring their father out on a winter's night during the darkest time of the year. He did not greet them, nor did any of his sons expect it. When he gestured for the other shepherds to come closer, the youngest son breathed a sigh of relief. If something had happened to his sister—or mother or any of the others, for that matter—his father would not have wished for the others to hear.

"This star that you've been going on about." His father looked directly at the shepherd boy, who felt the blood rush to his face. Now he was in trouble for talking about the star. He saw the brother next to him in age smirk. But it vanished at their father's next words.

"There is something to it."

As one, they all gazed up into the sky. Over the past days, the star no longer disappeared during the daylight, merely dimming in the presence of the sun, and now that the sun was setting, it was growing stronger by the moment. They all watched the light gain power; everything was so silent that the shepherd boy could hear their collective breathing.

Even the sheep were quiet, as though waiting for his father's news.

"Word has come from Jerusalem. Magi have appeared, following the star, saying it heralds the birth of the king of the Jews, king of kings. Some say the Lord God's Messiah."

A small, low sound escaped from the eldest shepherd and he turned away from them so that they could not see his face. After a moment, he raised his eyes once more to the star and did not look at them again.

The shepherd boy felt his own breath catch in his throat as his father continued. "Herod courted the wise ones, but they left him hurriedly and he cannot find them. They say he is mad with worry and anger."

The shepherd boy's oldest brother said, "That fox has been mad from birth."

His father answered, "But now his madness looks upon Bethlehem."

"Why Bethlehem?" asked one of the shepherds who had a young wife and infant child in the city.

"His scholars have assured him that Scripture points to David's city as the birthplace of the Messiah. His rage is up against the city."

The boy could not help himself. "What about our sister?"

His father turned a cold eye upon him. "Better to ask about your mother and brothers. If your sister had married, she would not be working at the inn in the city."

"But what does it mean?" pursued the shepherd with the wife and child in Bethlehem.

It had been a long time before his father had answered.

"God knows."

That had been hours past and now night had them in its grip, though the star and the mists it called forth with its heat lent a glow both sharp and eerie upon them. Even the sheep were restless, refusing to lie down and bleating fearfully. None of the shepherds slept, least of all the youngest, who felt that his very skin tingled with excitement and anxiety. There had been silence after his father had departed, but for once he understood. What was there to be said about something none of them could understand?

Suddenly, before their very eyes, the mists above them started to shimmer and intensify and, then, take shape. He was mesmerized; they all were. Had he been able to tear his eyes away from the sight before him, he would have seen even his disdainful brothers watching with fear and disbelief. Without knowing what they were doing, every shepherd, beginning with the youngest, sank to his knees. The shape before them could only be what they'd only heard described in Scripture readings.

An angel!

A man of God, yet not a man at all, but a creature of God able to assume the form of a man for the purpose of communicating with men! The shepherd boy found himself unable to draw breath. Every one of the sheep had gone silent, and he heard only the hoarse gasps of the eldest shepherd. From their knees they fell on their faces, though the shepherd boy kept his eyes on the angel, even when all others were too terrified to look. He saw an expression of mercy come over the angel's features, and, and, and, could it be?

Yes! Amusement! The angel, beautiful beyond all words known to all shepherds and scribes combined, smiled upon their abject terror.

And when the angel spoke, declaring and confirming the speculation the boy's father had described—that the Messiah they had been awaiting since the beginning of the Jews, the beginning of time, was born in Bethlehem—they heard the words clearly.

But the angel said to them, "Do not be afraid; for see—I am bringing you good news of great joy for all the people: to you is born this day in the city of David a Savior, who is the Messiah, the Lord. This will be a sign for you: you will find a child wrapped in bands of cloth and lying in a manger" [Luke 2:10–12].

But the boy heard something oddly familiar in the voice of the angel who declared God's message. He searched all the memories of his fevered mind until he understood. The angel's voice sounded like the music the boy thought of as coming from the star, music he'd heard only in his dreams from the day the star first appeared. And the angel, seeing the dawning of comprehension on the boy's face, smiled upon him.

Then, for what seemed an eternity of fearful ecstasy to the shepherds, the mists congealed into unnumbered angels who lifted their voices in a song of praise that both petrified them and made them weep with grief when it finally stopped.

When it did, and when the star was all that was left in the now-lightening sky, the shepherd boy was the first one on his feet, running down to Bethlehem. His brothers were right behind him.

PRAY

Beloved Lord Jesus, I live in a world where so many people claim to know all about you. They interpret the signs of the times, they explain Scripture, they declare what it is you would have the world, nations, states, communities, and even individuals do. Just as your star caused many to wonder and speculate and make proclamations, so today do people seek—and sometimes announce—the meaning of all things attached to you. Some even dare to speak their own interpretations and opinions in your name. People go to war in your name, Lord. People have supported slavery in your name, Lord. These days, people write elaborate novels, and series of novels, describing what the future will be for those who believe in you. Just as people over 2,000 years ago looked for signs, so it is today. Lord, as your birthday comes upon me, teach me humility. Remind me that because I am only human, I cannot hope to probe the recesses of your vast, magnificent, and unknowable intelligence. Protect me from the kind of arrogance that declares an opinion as a truth and seeks comfort in interpretations. This Christmas and always, Jesus, help me to humbly center myself on the indis-

putable message of your birth, life, death, and resurrection: Love. Amen.

ACT

Beginning today be a light to the world as Jesus asks of his apostles and disciples. Become a human version of the star that heralded Jesus' coming. Every day, seek to do one thing that is kind, loving, helpful, illuminating. Try not to let a day slip by without doing something, no matter how small. Make sure someone gets a piece of their mail that was mistakenly delivered to you. Greet a stranger. Greet a neighbor. Move a newspaper that was tossed in a driveway up to the doorstep. Knock on a door to let the owner know they've left the lights on in their car. Pray for the person who cuts you off in traffic. Pray for the teacher who is making your child unhappy. Point out a full moon or a rainbow to someone who is missing it. Or a star! The list is endless. Your time is not. Start today. You will bring the joy of Christmas to every day of the year.

QUESTIONS

1. What is your first memory of the Christmas Star? How was the story explained to you?

2. Do angels speak to us today, as individuals? As God's people? What, if any, are today's angelic messages and how do they come to us?

OTHER TITLES *by* MARCI ALBORGHETTI

When Lightning Strikes Twice
This book explores the wide range of thoughts and feelings that come when a crisis returns. It examines how people in the grip of repeated tragedy experienced the event, faced their circumstances, learned to cope, and found their way to a stronger faith and deeper trust in God.

152 PAGES | $12.95 | 978-1-58595-378-3

12 Strong Women of God
Biblical Models for Today
Stories of women larger than life, yet who were vulnerable and in need of God's loving aid—these are the stories you'll find here. Both women and men who read these stories will recognize some of the challenges they face in their own lives. They can take courage from the example of the biblical heroines Marci writes about in such an insightful and easy-to-read style.

136 PAGES | $12.95 | 978-1-58595-326-4

The Jesus Women
These twelve extraordinary first-person narratives are from women who were contemporaries of Jesus Christ—and their stories make for great Lenten reading. Each woman experienced him in a unique way and each became a disciple in her own right. The stories are drawn from Scripture and invite a personal response through an "Active Meditation" and a series of pertinent reflection questions.

136 PAGES | $14.95 | 978-1-58595-576-3

TWENTY THIRD
PUBLICATIONS

1-800-321-0411
WWW.23RDPUBLICATIONS.COM